Foreword

I'm delighted to have the opportunity to write the introduction to this serie of first-class guides from Lil Publications, because Wales has alway held a very special place in m affections.

That's no doubt due in part to t strong Celtic connections between the Irish and the Welsh. In both countries the Celtic influence is still strong - one of the chief ingredients in the potent mixture of myth and magic that today gives Wales its uniquely enchanting character and appeal.

My love of Wales has increased over the years, as both business and pleasure have brought me back on many occasions. The more I see of it, the more I appreciate what an enormous diversity of landscape is packed into such a small area. From the misty mountains of Snowdonia to the golden beaches of Gower, Wales contrives to present you with a different view at every turn of the road. Yet it all enjoys the same indefinable quality - which in some mysterious way, I feel, speaks volumes for the marvellous Welsh language.

But enough of my meandering! You're reading this because you want to discover a particular area of Wales for yourself. Well, I guarantee you'll find this excellent guide crammed with useful information to help you make the

most of your visit.

And with other titles available in this series, covering different but equally beautiful parts of Wales, I'm pretty sure that before long you'll be back for more!

Happy holiday.

Gloria Hunniford

Introduction

This new visitor guide stands alone as the only publication to bring together in one volume six holidays areas of south-west Wales - Llanelli, Swansea Bay & Mumbles, the Gower Peninsula, the Vale of Neath, Port Talbot & the Afan Valley, and Porthcawl & Ogwr.

Some, notably Gower and Swansea Bay, are already well established as popular holiday destinations. Others, such as Llanelli and Port Talbot, will come as something of a surprise to readers who are of the impression that these are places renowned only for their factories, coal mines and urban sprawl.

The truth is that every one of the six areas described in these pages has a great deal to offer. Landscapes decimated by decades of industry and mining have been successfully reclaimed. Even Port Talbot's steelworks, not a pretty sight viewed from the M4, are only a few miles from one of Wales' most picturesque attractions - the beautiful Afan Valley.

As you will discover, this guide is packed with delights. Superb beaches, magnificent coastlines, enchanting waterfalls, wooded valleys, forested hills, vast country parks, first-class leisure and sporting facilities, and holiday attractions of every description - they are all here, and much more besides.

Above all this book is intended as a practical, quick-reference guide to appeal to visitors and locals alike. History and other background reading is here if you want it, but essential information such as attractions, places of interest and recreational facilities are listed and described separately at the end of each section. A great deal of time and care has gone into compiling this information, which to the best of the author's knowledge was correct at the time of going to press.

This is the fourth title in the series of visitor guides from Lily Publications. The other titles are

Pembrokeshire & South West Wales
Ceredigion and the Aberystwyth Coast
The Isle of Man

All are available from good bookshops or direct from Lily Publications, at the address shown on page 96.

John F Hendy

View across Loughor Estuary

SWANSEA BAY 94/95
Gower & Llanelli Coast Guide

WRITTEN AND EDITED BY TREVOR BARRETT

CONTENTS

FOREWORD 3
by Gloria Hunniford

INTRODUCTION 4

THE GREAT BEACH HOLIDAY 5
(Your quick-reference beach guide)

LLANELLI'S GOLDEN COAST 13

SWANSEA BAY & MUMBLES 23

THE GOWER PENINSULA 38

THE VALE OF NEATH 49

PORT TALBOT & THE AFAN VALLEY ..66

PORTHCAWL & OGWR 77

EXPLORING FURTHER AFIELD 85

THE NATIONAL TRUST 91

ACCOMMODATION & EATING OUT 93

INDEX 94

TOURIST INFORMATION CENTRES 96

ACKNOWLEDGEMENTS 96

AREA MAP 42-43

TOWN PLANS

Llanelli 16

Swansea City Centre 24

The Mumbles 35

Port Talbot.................................67

Porthcawl..................................79

All accommodation participates in the Wales Tourist Board's inspection scheme. If readers have any concern about the standards of any accommodation, please take the matter up directly with the provider of the accommodation, as soon as possible. Failing satisfaction, please contact the Wales Tourist Board, Development Services Unit, Brunel House, 2 Fitzalan Road, Cardiff CF2 1UY.

Published by Lily Publications, 12 Millfields Close, Pentlepoir, Kilgetty, Pembrokeshire, Wales SA68 0SA. Tel: (0834) 811895, Fax: (0834) 814484.

A Cottage on Gower

The Great Beach Holiday

The stretches of South Wales coastline described in this guide boast an abundance of superb beaches. In fact, there are all kinds of beaches for all kinds of people.

Wide, safe, sandy beaches for children and families.

Secluded, quiet coves and small bays where you can relax in peace.

And beaches for surfers, windsurfers, water-skiers, canoeists and sailing enthusiasts.

Regular tests are carried out to ensure that bathing water quality around the most popular and accessible beaches meets EEC standards. Some beaches are also declared dog-free zones during summer months for reasons of safety and hygiene.

The following is a quick guide to the region's beaches, four of which won important awards in 1993. Some of the facilities described are applicable during the summer season only - in particular lifeguard patrols, regular bus services and beach shops and cafes.

CEFN SIDAN SANDS, PEMBREY

This is a truly magnificent stretch of golden sands - 7 miles in all, including the southern extension of Pembrey beach - and in 1993 it not only won a Premier Resort Award from the Tidy Britain Group, but also a European Blue Flag Award. The beach is backed by dunes and the attractive conservation area of Pembrey Country Park, which offers nature trails, walks, picnics, cafes and restaurant, and a host of sports and activities such as the dry ski slope. The beach, which is safe for swimming and good for surfing, is well monitored by the park's ranger service, and in summer there is also a lifeguard patrol. As with the beach at Pembrey, the facilities here are equal to those of an established seaside resort because of the very extensive amenities and attractions of the country park.

PEMBREY

The beach at Pembrey, accessible through the country park, is a southern extension of award-winning Cefn Sidan Sands, which curve round towards Burry Port. Treacherous currents make bathing unsafe at the mouth of the Loughor estuary. There is a golf course set in the sand dunes nearby, and Burry Port itself has a launching slipway and harbour and is popular with boating enthusiasts. Facilities are extensive because of the proximity of Pembrey Country Park, which is described on page 18.

LLANELLI

You have to travel through an area of industrial estate and disused dockland to reach it, but Llanelli beach is a pleasant surprise to those who make the effort. It is a long beach with superb views over the Loughor estuary and the northern shoreline of Gower, and at low tide there is a vast stretch of exposed sand. Facilities: easy but limited parking, easy access to the beach.

SWANSEA BAY

Miles of wide sands stretching from the Maritime Quarter to the Mumbles, and backed by all the leisure, sports and shopping amenities of Wales' second largest city. The bay is used mainly for recreational purposes - such as windsurfing, fishing, canoeing, sailing and water-skiing - rather than for bathing. Parts of the beach are designated dog-free zones during the summer. Facilities: toilets, regular bus service, parking, shops along the promenade, easy access.

Sunday morning watersports at Oxwich

John F Hendy

THE MUMBLES

Standing at the western tip of the wide sweep of Swansea Bay, Mumbles has a long promenade, a Victorian pier with a small fun fair and amusements, Mumbles Head lighthouse, and the famous Mumbles Mile of shops, pubs and restaurants. The beach is popular for recreation and watersports. Other facilities: toilets, regular bus service, parking, deck chair hire, launching slipways, easy access.

BRACELET BAY, GOWER

A small cove with pebbles and rock pools. Popular for canoeing, fishing, walking and Mumbles Hill Local Nature Reserve. There is a beach shop cafe at nearby Limeslade Bay. Facilities: lifeguard patrol, toilets (abled and disabled), telephone, regular bus service, parking, steps to beach.

LIMESLADE BAY, GOWER

A rocky cove with sand exposed at low tide. Popular for fishing and swimming. Rescue Aids are sited on the beach. Other facilities: toilets (abled and disabled), regular bus service, parking, beach shop, steps to beach.

ROTHERSLADE & LANGLAND, GOWER

Though part of the same bay, these two beaches are separated at high tide, Langland being the larger and very popular with families. At low tide there is a fine stretch of sandy beach, fringed by beach huts. The bay is a popular venue for golf and tennis as well as for swimming, surfing and fishing. Both beaches are designated dog-free zones during summer months, and Langland is a popular surfing beach. Facilities: lifeguard patrol, toilets (abled and disabled), telephone, regular bus service, parking, beach shops and cafes, deckchair hire, steps to beaches.

CASWELL BAY, GOWER

A large and popular sandy beach, well patronised by families, and set in a very picturesque bay. An added attraction is Bishop's Wood Nature Reserve in Caswell Valley. The beach is ideal for swimming, surfing, windsurfing, fishing and canoeing, and is a dog-free zone in summer.

Facilities: deckchair hire, toilets, telephone, regular bus service, parking, beach shop, easy access.

BRANDY COVE, GOWER

A secluded sandy cove with rocks and pebbles, once notorious for smuggling. This is a good beach for swimming and fishing, but its isolated location means a long walk from the main road. Facilities: regular bus service, shops in Bishopston village.

PWLL-DU BAY, GOWER

A large, secluded sandy beach backed by a high bank of pebbles, through which a stream from the beautiful Bishopston Valley enters the sea. There is a long walk to this isolated beach from the main road, but once here you can enjoy good swimming and fishing. Facilities: regular bus service, shops in Bishopston village.

PEBBLES BAY, GOWER

This pebble and sand beach, which is covered at high tide, is also in an isolated spot and can only be reached after a long walk from the main road. Facilities: regular bus service to the villages of Southgate and Parkmill, which offer shops and parking.

TOR BAY, GOWER

A sandy beach lying west of the Great Tor rock at the eastern end of Oxwich Bay. Facilities: regular bus service to the nearest village of Penmaen, which also offers limited parking, but the walk to the beach is long and difficult and access is down a steep path.

PENMAEN SANDS, GOWER

As with Tor Bay, access to Penmaen Sands involves a long walk and steep descent. The reward is that this sandy beach, located to the west of Three Cliffs Bay, is very often deserted. Close by are several historic sites, including the remains of Penmaen Old Castle, a megalithic tomb and a church. According to legend a lost village lies buried beneath the sands. Facilities: regular bus service to Penmaen, where there is also limited parking.

Three Cliffs Bay from Pennard

THREE CLIFFS BAY, GOWER

One of the most picturesque bays on the Gower Peninsula, with spectacular views. The ruins of Pennard Castle overlook the valley, down which a tidal stream runs into the sea, creating dangerous currents. Facilities: telephone, regular bus services to the villages of Southgate and Parkmill (which also have shops and parking), and access to the beach only after a long walk from either village.

CRAWLEY, GOWER

Another isolated beach which can only be reached after a long walk from Nicholaston Cross, to which there is a regular bus service.

OXWICH BAY, GOWER

One of the most popular family beaches on Gower, with a long stretch of golden sand. In summer there are guided walks through the Nature Reserve. Within the reserve are most of the dunes, marshes and woods skirting Oxwich Sands. This is also a popular venue for sailing, water-skiing, fishing and canoeing, and windsurfing tuition and hire are available. Facilities: boat slip, toilets, regular bus service, parking, beach shops and cafes, and easy access.

HORTON, GOWER

A sandy beach sheltered by the huge sand dunes which link it to Port-Eynon. Horton is a popular spot for watersports and fishing, and there are lifeguards at Port-Eynon. Facilities: toilets (abled and disabled), regular bus service, parking, shops near beach, easy access.

Below: Oxwich Bay

John F Hendy

PORT-EYNON, GOWER

Port-Eynon is one of the star attractions of Gower, with a large sandy beach and excellent facilities. It also currently holds a Premier Rural Beach Award from the Tidy Britain Group - the highest accolade offered under the Group's well-publicised Seaside Awards scheme, and made in recognition of Port-Eynon's high standards of water quality, beach cleanliness and safety. The beach is not only very popular with bathers but also with enthusiasts of windsurfing, canoeing and boating. Facilities: lifeguard patrol, youth hostel, toilets (abled and disabled), regular bus service, parking, beach shops and cafes, windsurfing hire, boat slip, and easy access.

MEWSLADE BAY, GOWER

A secluded and isolated sandy beach set amongst magnificent cliff scenery west of Thurba Head. Facilities: regular bus service to Pitton or parking in a private farm field, but access to the beach requires a long and difficult walk.

FALL BAY, GOWER

An extension of Mewslade Bay, this secluded sandy beach is covered at high tide. Its isolated location south of Rhossili means that access is only possible after a long walk.

RHOSSILI BAY, GOWER

Considered by many to be one of the finest beaches in Wales, if not Britain. The village of Rhossili is dramatically poised on a cliff 200 feet above the superb crescent of sand, with magnificent views over the outstretched finger of the Worms Head peninsula and the huge sweep of Carma 'hen Bay to the west.

The beach offers excellent bathing and is also very popular for surfing, canoeing, hang-gliding and fishing. Access to Worms Head is restricted to four hours either side of low tide.

Facilities: National Trust shop and Information Centre, toilets (abled and disabled), a regular bus service, large private car park, and shops in Rhossili village. Access to the beach is via a long steep walk from the village.

LLANGENNITH, GOWER

An extension of Rhossili Bay, Llangennith is acknowledged as one of Britain's premier surfing beaches and is a favourite spot for swimming, canoeing and fishing. At low tide you can cross the sand to the island of Burry Holms and discover the remains of a medieval monastic settlement. Away from the beach, the village of Llangennith also attracts visitors; the well-known Gower folk singer Phil Tanner is buried in the churchyard here. Beach facilities: toilets, bus service, large private car park, shops on the caravan site in the village, easy access to the beach.

BLUEPOOL BAY, GOWER

A sandy cove accessible only on foot from Llangennith or Broughton Bay. The bay is a dangerous bathing area and gets its name from the circular rock pool at the foot of the cliffs, in which bathing is not recommended either. Facilities: regular bus service to Llangennith and parking at Broughton Bay, but access to the beach is extremely difficult.

BROUGHTON BAY, GOWER

Fringed by the sand dunes of Broughton Burrows, this large sandy beach runs into Whiteford Sands towards the mouth of the Loughor estuary. The treacherous currents of the estuary mean that bathing here is dangerous both at low water mark and on the outgoing tide, but by way of compensation the cliff-top views are dramatic. Facilities: bus service to Llangennith, where there is a private car park and a caravan site offering shops, toilets and easy access to the beach.

WHITEFORD SANDS, GOWER

This beautiful sandy beach extends to Whiteford Point - the most northerly point on Gower and the site of a disused lighthouse. The beach is backed by Whiteford Burrows and together they form part of a National Nature Reserve. As with the adjacent beach of Broughton Bay, bathing here is dangerous because of treacherous estuary currents. Facilities: bus service to Llanmadoc, with easy access to the beach from the caravan site.

ABERAVON, PORT TALBOT

Two miles of sands, a promenade and the sports and leisure facilities of Afon Lido have made Aberavon a popular destination for day trippers over the years. Now a major redevelopment of the entire Aberavon seafront is under way. This will include a new golf course, modernisation and extension of Afan Lido, and rejuvenation of the beach itself. See page 70 for further information and details of facilities.

MARGAM SANDS, PORT TALBOT

A large expanse of sand lying to the south of Port Talbot docks and backed by the dunes of Margam Burrows and the less welcome spread of Port Talbot's infamous steelworks. The proximity of the works has tended to overshadow the fact that Margam is a superb beach, stretching south for several miles and running into Kenfig Sands and burrows. To the east are all the attractions and picturesque scenery of Margam Country Park.

REST BAY, PORTHCAWL

A small bay which at low tide boasts an inviting expanse of clean golden sand and several rock pools. The beach is very popular with surfers, and lifeguards are on duty during the peak summer months. Superb cliff-top walks are an added attraction. In 1993 Rest Bay won a Rural Seaside Award from the Tidy Britain Group.

SANDY BAY AND TRECCO BAY

These two beaches, with wide expanses of safe golden sands and an abundance of rock pools, are very popular with families. Each also has a caravan park sited adjacent to the beach, and nearby are all the resort amenities of Porthcawl itself and the fun and attractions of Coney Beach Pleasure Park. The beaches offer safe bathing and are patrolled by lifeguards in the summer season.

MERTHYR MAWR, PORTHCAWL

A haven of peace and tranquility, this is an area of high grassy sand dunes rather than beach, though it does extend between low hills and the sea. A designated SSSI - Site of Special Scientific Interest.

OGMORE-BY-SEA, NR PORTHCAWL

Attractively located at the mouth of the River Ogmore, the sandy beach is fringed with areas of grass. However, estuary currents make bathing here dangerous. Facilities include easy parking near the shore, and cafes.

SOUTHERNDOWN, NR OGMORE

A popular surfing bay, Southerndown is full of character and at low tide has a wide expanse of clean golden sand and an abundance of rock pools. Fine views are enhanced by cliff-top walks. Facilities: limited parking, lifeguards, Heritage Coast Visitor Centre. In 1993 Southerdown won a Rural Beach Award from the Tidy Britain Group.

The Seaside Awards

In 1993, four beaches in the region qualified for an award from the Tidy Britain Group, as part of their well-publicised Seaside Award initiative.

Environmentalists, however, are opposed to awards such as these because they maintain that the standards of water quality which apply, as stipulated by the EC (EU) Bathing Water Directive, are not high enough. Certainly, the whole question of water quality has become a complex and contentious issue - not only around the shores of Britain and Europe, but worldwide.

On the other hand, it can be argued that the Seaside Awards are a very positive step in helping to ensure higher standards of cleanliness and safety on Britain's beaches.

As the Tidy Britain Group points out, not everyone who spends time on the beach will venture into the sea. Many holidaymakers are content to sunbathe, relax, play beach games with the children or explore rock pools. So water quality is not the be all and end all; the quality and cleanliness of the beach itself are equally important.

And this is why each Seaside Award is made on the basis of the standards achieved by both.

What exactly is the Seaside Award?

The Seaside Award was introduced in 1992 to encourage higher standards of cleanliness, water quality and safety on Britain's beaches. The award recognises two distinct categories of beach - rural and resort - and is made for a twelve-month period, during which time the successful beach is entitled to fly the blue and yellow Seaside Award flag. When the twelve months expire, the local authority must re-apply to the Tidy Britain Group. The beach will be completely reassessed and granted another Seaside Award for the next twelve-month period only if it satisfies all the criteria.

How does a beach win a Seaside Award?

To qualify for a Seaside Award, a rural beach must satisfy the Tidy Britain Group that both the beach itself and the bathing water meet the required standards. This means that the beach has to be free of litter, industrial waste, sewage-related debris, oil pollution and large accumulations of rotting seaweed.

As for water quality, this must meet the mandatory ("good") standard of the EC Bathing Water Directive. However, should the water quality achieve the much higher guideline ("excellent") standard of the EC Directive, the beach qualifies for a Premier Seaside Award. In either case, the water must be sampled and tested at least 20 times a year. Beaches with a Seaside Award fly a pale blue and yellow flag; those with a Premier Seaside Award fly a dark blue and yellow flag.

Resorts, of course, are much busier than rural beaches, and for any resort to win a Seaside Award (as did Cefn Sidan Sands, Pembrey, in 1993) it has to satisfy no less than 29 different criteria! These include good housekeeping and management, safety, and the provision of regularly updated information.

So clearly, any beach or resort which flies the Seaside Award flag is making a big effort to clean up its act. The flag, in fact, symbolises a commitment by the local authority to maintain the high standards it has worked so hard to achieve.

And that has to be good news for everybody who wants to enjoy our beaches.

Llanelli's Golden Coast

For a town which was once the tinplate capital of the world, and whose prosperity has been forged from the spoils of heavy industry, Llanelli comes as a pleasant surprise to the first-time visitor. Several surprises, in fact.

The first is the realisation that Llanelli is not only a town; it is also a borough, created in 1913 and extending over 90 square miles. Within its boundaries are Burry Port, Pembrey, Kidwelly, and many attractions which have established the area as a growing centre of tourism and leisure. Foremost among these are the vast Pembrey Country Park, the award-winning Penclacwydd Wildfowl & Wetlands Centre, Pembrey Motorsports Centre and Kidwelly Castle.

Llanelli's location certainly works in its favour. It stands on the beautiful Loughor estuary, on the eastern seaboard of Carmarthen Bay. All within very easy reach are the magnificent 7-mile stretch of Cefn Sidan Sands, the shops and entertainment of Swansea, the spectacular beaches and scenery of the Gower Peninsula, and the wild and unspoilt splendour of the Brecon Beacons National Park.

Llanelli's second big surprise is the town itself. Though home to a population of over 35,000 people - the highest of any town in Dyfed - it enjoys a relaxing and unhurried atmosphere, particularly in the pedestrianised shopping centre. Here you will find many familiar High Street names and a good choice of places to eat. Barely a mile away, at Parc Trostre, is the most westerly McDonald's restaurant currently to be found in the whole of South and West Wales.

The town also has a bustling daily indoor market, and is well known in Wales for its twice-weekly open air market (main market day Thursday, also open Saturday).

Another unexpected feature of Llanelli is its spread of attractive parks and gardens. Sandy Water Park, People's Park, Parc Howard and other places offer relaxation in very pleasant surroundings. On the other hand, if excitement is

Parc Howard, Llanelli

Wales Tourist Board

your craving, there's one park you really shouldn't miss - Stradey Park, home of Llanelli Rugby Football Club, on a Saturday afternoon. The Scarlets are one of Britain's most successful club sides and a familiar name to rugby fans around the world. The club's rugby posts are adorned with saucepans - a tribute to the boisterous local anthem "Sospan Fach" (The Little Saucepan) which was Llanelli's trademark.

Stradey Park also has a museum depicting the history of the club, and it is open to visitors by arrangement.

For those who prefer to participate rather than spectate, Llanelli offers impressive sports facilities - not least the superb new indoor complex of Llanelli Leisure Centre. This brings together under one roof the Jubilee Pool, large sports hall, purpose-built registered creche, state-of-the-art fitness gym and much more, as described on page 21. Entertainment, on the other hand, is available at the multi-screen cinema of Theatre Elli.

But Llanelli's biggest surprise of all is its beach. The three-quarters of a mile drive from the centre of the town takes you through the least picturesque part of Llanelli - the old North Docks - but the effort is well rewarded. The beach is long and sandy, and at low tide a vast area of sand and saltmarsh is exposed that seems to stretch right across the Loughor estuary to the beckoning Gower Peninsula. Views over the estuary, and along the near coastline towards Burry Port and Pembrey, are superb. Oystercatchers and curlews frequent the beach, as do an increasing number of holidaymakers throughout the summer months.

Glimpses of the past

Like much of South Wales today, Llanelli has undergone a metamorphosis as traditional industries have faded away and leisure and tourism have blossomed.

Such a transition is nothing new in the town's history. Though coal was mined in Llanelli and Kidwelly as early as 1536, Llanelli was still only a village until the mid-18th century. Yet just one hundred years later, the unstoppable advance of the Industrial Revolution had changed the place beyond recognition.

The transformation began with the sudden and rapid development of the iron industry. Early in the 19th century, Alexander Raby opened the Furnace ironworks north of the town, and followed this by building the first modern dock and the Dafen works, which opened in 1847. The harbour was a hive of activity as iron, coal, tinplate and then steel production flourished. Chimneys shaped the skyline and many small tinplate works prospered in the hands of craftsmen.

The story of those industrious days in Llanelli's history is retold in the Tinplate Industry Museum at Trostre and in the museum at Parc Howard.

Between 1840 and 1925, Llanelli was also famous for its pottery. Examples of the craft are now on show in the pottery collection at the Parc Howard Gallery.

Llanelli firsts

Llanelli is home to two breweries - Felinfoel and Buckleys - and was the first town to put beer into cans.

Another local innovation was the spare wheel, which was patented by a Llanelli family.

And Llanelli had the first Welsh language school, and the first music library.

The welcome face of Llanelli

Modern Llanelli is a town which is meeting the challenges of a changing world. It is attracting new and diverse industries, located to the east of the town, and many new visitors who are drawn by the realisation that here is an ideal holiday base for discovering South and West Wales.

Access by road (M4) and rail (mainline InterCity) could not be better. And with its excellent choice of attractions, entertainment, sports and leisure facilities and beautiful beaches, Llanelli's golden coast offers a very warm welcome.

As the borough's tourist brochure says, there is never a dull day here.

ATTRACTIONS & PLACES OF INTEREST

Penclacwydd Wildfowl & Wetlands Centre

Which migrating swan is capable of flying as high as Everest in temperatures as low as minus 48° C? Why are flamingos pink, and why do they stand on one leg? Exactly how deep can a diving duck dive?

Whether or not you have ever pondered the answers to such intriguing questions, this award-winning centre offers a fascinating family day out. The only one of its kind in Wales, it was opened in 1991,designed by Sir Peter Scott and built by LLanelli Borough Council, who lease it to the Wildfowl & Wetlands Trust.

Popular with experts and sightseers alike, Penclacwydd is beautifully landscaped, and situated on the Loughor estuary. Two hundred acres of saltmarsh, watermeadow and estuary provide home to large numbers of wintering ducks and waders, which are best seen from the purpose-built hides. The views are spectacular as flocks of curlew, oystercatcher and redshank wheel over the saltmarsh.

The centre has a resident population of more than 1100 wildfowl originating from all over the world. These include black-necked swans, the rare and endangered white-winged wood duck, and Caribbean flamingos. Small birds of prey are seen here too, such as peregrine falcons, kestrels and short-eared owls, along with herons and kingfishers.

A visit to Penclacwydd Wildfowl & Wetlands Centre is a wonderful opportunity to get close to nature and to make a valuable contribution to conservation at the same time, as all admission money goes directly to conserving wetland environments. The centre has excellent facilities for both able-bodied and disabled visitors, with easy paths for pushchairs, a baby room, wheelchair access to most areas - including the hides - and free parking. There is also a gift and book shop, an exhibition area, a coffee shop/cafe serving up home-cooked food and great views, and a Visitor Centre. Why not round off your visit by becoming a member of the Wildfowl & Wetlands Trust, or even adopting a duck or a swan?

The centre is open all year round and offers low-price family tickets. It is 3 miles east of Llanelli, just off the A484 Swansea road. From the M4 take junction 47 or 48.

Sandy Water Park

Standing at the highest point in the park and taking in the views over Carmarthen Bay and Gower, you would hardly believe that for many years this was the site of a huge steelworks. But today work has

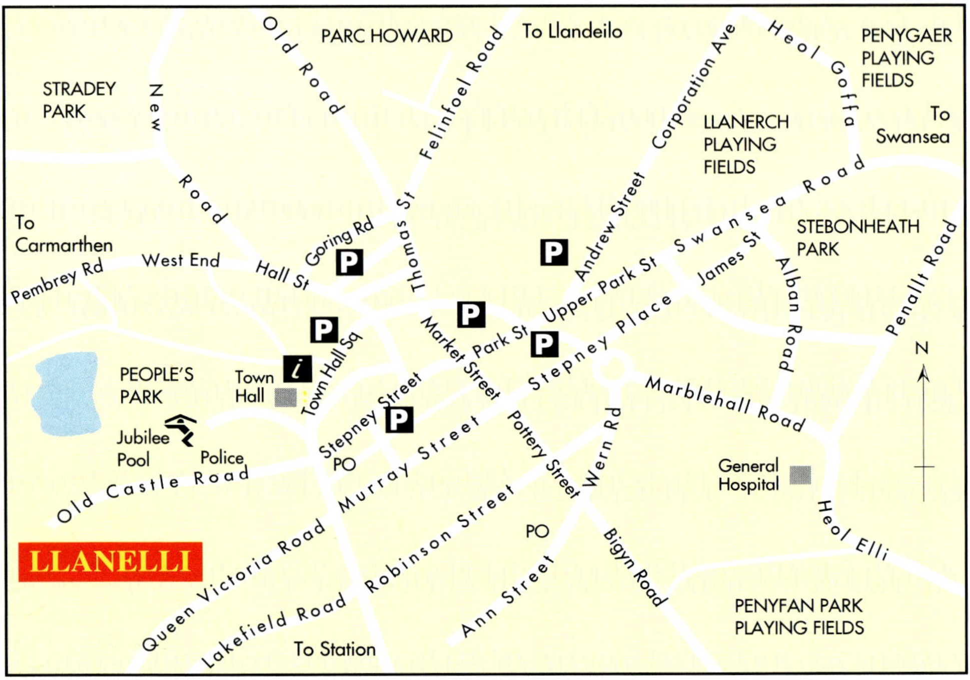

given way to play. The park's centre of attraction is a 16-acre lake which offers plenty of opportunities for watersports, and there are pleasant landscaped walkways with access to Llanelli beach.

Swiss Valley

Swiss Valley is the beautiful area around the Upper and Lower Lliedi reservoirs, just to the north of Llanelli. Woodland walks, wildlife, trout fishing and relaxation are the big attractions here.

The Furnace

Just north of Llanelli, on the outskirts of the town, is the 19th-century iron furnace which gave this village its name. The iron industry thrived in Llanelli and the furnace was worked round the clock to produce cannon and cannon balls for the Napoleonic wars. The furnace was built by Alexander Raby and is now a listed building.

Furnace Pond

The furnace (see above) stands near the entrance to this recently-developed leisure area, which originally was the 5-million-gallon Trebeddrod Reservoir, built in 1854 to supply water to Llanelli. Now known as Furnace Pond, it is an ideal spot for country walks, fishing, and strolling through the landscaped Japanese water garden. An excellent leaflet describing the Furnace Pond Nature Trail is available from Llanelli's Tourist Information Centre.

Parc Howard

Just a short walk from Llanelli town centre, Parc Howard is an ornamental park which features trees unusual to Britain. Attractions in the park include extensive playing fields, playgrounds, bowling greens, tennis courts and the Gorsedd Circle of stones, erected for the 1930 National Eisteddfod. In the centre of the park is the Mansion House, the former home of local benefactor Sir Stafford Howard and now home to Llanelli Museum. Here you will find an interesting collection of paintings, examples of early local tinplate, and a display of the now rare Llanelli pottery. The house and park were presented to the town by Sir Stafford Howard, Llanelli's first mayor, and opened to the public in 1912.

People's Park

Also known as Parc Y Dre, People's Park is virtually in Llanelli town centre, to the rear of the impressive neo-Jacobean Town Hall, which celebrates its centenary in 1996. Here you will find the excellent new Llanelli Leisure Centre (described on page 21), as well as attractive gardens, a playground and paddling pool, and a bowling green and tennis courts.

Llanelli Entertainment Centre

A three-screen cinema open six days a week (Tuesday to Sunday inclusive) and offering the very best in new and classic films, as well as amateur and professional stage productions.

Llanelli Market

Get a real taste of Llanelli at the open air Thursday market - a weekly tradition here since the 15th century. Among the many things on offer is a very tempting choice of fresh local produce, including fish, cockles, vegetables, Welsh cheeses, laver bread and other delicacies. The market, also open on Saturdays, is in addition to the daily indoor market.

The Mill

Embedded in the pavement in Prospect Place, Llanelli, is an old mill stone - another and permanent reminder of the town's industrious past.

The Library

Llanelli town library is of historical interest for two reasons. One is the memorial to John Wesley, who visited Llanelli to preach on eight different occasions between 1768 and 1788. The other is the library's Victorian wall letterbox, which is the oldest in Llanelli. The library is one of the best in South Wales, with a music library unrivalled for its range and quality.

Dai the Dragon's Adventure World

Described as Llanelli's biggest and brightest indoor adventure playground, this supervised play centre provides fun and entertainment for all children aged 1-12. Parents can relax in the coffee shop while the youngsters enjoy everything from the enormous ball pool and giant tube slide to the inflatable dragons and aerial runway. And afterwards, there's also the promise of dragon burgers in Dai's burger bar. The centre is conveniently located in Town Hall Square, Llanelli.

Pembrey & Burry Port

Situated just west of Llanelli, on the A484 Carmarthen road, the area around Pembrey and Burry Port is very well known for two of the region's major tourist attractions - Pembrey Country Park, which includes part of the magnificent 7-mile stretch of Cefn Sidan Sands, and the Welsh Motorsports Centre.

But Burry Port has other claims to fame. It was here that the waterproof material used in the making of the Mackintosh was discovered by chance at the town's copperworks, when a piece of green baize from a worker's apron accidentally fell into a vat and became waterproofed during the coppermaking process!

And Burry Port featured in world headlines on June 18th 1928 when the first aircraft to cross the Atlantic non-stop, the seaplane *Friendship*, splashed down near the harbour after a 23-hour flight. The pilot was Commander Stulz, and his passenger, Miss Amelia Earhart, became the first woman to make the Atlantic crossing by air. Memorials to this historic event can be seen in Burry Port harbour and the George Inn, in Stepney Road.

ATTRACTIONS & PLACES OF INTEREST

Burry Port Harbour

The harbour at Burry Port, built in the days when the coal and tinplate industries were thriving, is now well patronised by yachts, pleasure craft and fishermen. The annual Fishing Festival attracts anglers from all over the UK and offers excellent prizes and entertainment. From the quayside wall there are superb views over the estuary to Gower, and west of the harbour are Ashburnham golf links and the sands, dunes and burrows of Cefn Sidan.

St. Illtyd's Church, Pembrey

The 13th-century church is the oldest building in the area, and in the churchyard is a memorial to those who drowned when the French ship *Jeune Emma* ran aground on the treacherous Cefn Sidan Sands in 1828. Among the victims was Adeline Coqueline, who according to the inscription was "the niece of Josephine, Consort to the renowned individual Napoleon Bonaparte".

Cefn Sidan Beach, Pembrey Country Park

Y Ffald

Outside the church gates of St. Illtyd is a circle of stones attached to the church wall. This is a rare example of a medieval animal pound, where stray animals were impounded and eventually sold off to swell church funds if no one claimed them.

Pembrey Country Park

Owned and managed by Llanelli Borough Council, this top tourist attraction is a wonderful blend of coast and countryside. It occupies the site of the old Pembrey Royal Ordnance Factory - but you would never suspect it! There are over 500 acres of beautiful woods and grassland, fringed by one of the finest beaches in Europe. Cefn Sidan Sands has won the European Blue Flag Award every year since 1990, and the Premier Seaside Award in 1992, 1993 and 1994.

There is no admission charge to the park; you pay only for parking. The park is open all year round from dawn till dusk, and the facilities and attractions are first-class. There are toilets, mother and baby room, Visitor Centre and gift shop, free Easirider wheelchair service, special services for educational groups, restaurant, beach cafe, and picnic and barbecue areas. Things to do include an all-year-round dry ski slope, the brand new Cobra toboggan run (the longest in Wales), equestrian centre, falconry centre, 9-hole pitch & putt, narrow gauge and miniature railways, adventure playground, woodland nature trails and an orienteering course. A great day out in anyone's book!

The Welsh Motorsports Centre

The roar of the race track and the dash for the chequered flag never fail to enthral the crowds at Pembrey's famous motorsport venue. Set in 500 acres, the challenging circuit regularly hosts top competitive action on both two wheels and four, and is one of the leading motorsport attractions in Britain. A new feature is the Formula One bar and restaurant. The annual Welsh Festival of Motorsport, held in September, gives everyone the opportunity to try their hand at the wheel, at little or no cost. The festival also includes a full race programme, a motorshow, stalls and entertainment. Race meetings are held at Pembrey on most weekends between March and October, and highlights for the 1994 season include British Championship Rallycross, British Formula 3 and the British Truck Racing Championship.

LLANELLI

Pembrey Country Park

Cefn Sidan Blue Flag Beach

Penclacwydd Wildfowl & Wetlands Centre

Welsh Motor Sport Centre

- Pembrey Country Park - a combination of wooded parks and a wide variety of attractions including Llanelli's own Blue Flag Beach - Cefn Sidan.
- Welsh Motor Sport Centre - taste the excitement of sports events at the racing and rallying school.

WALES' GOLDEN COAST

Penclacwydd Wildfowl & Wetlands Centre

Kidwelly Castle

- Penclacwydd Wildfowl and Wetlands Centre - Come and observe the wide variety of wild and captive birds in their natural habitat.
- Kidwelly Castle - situated in spectacular settings, savour the views and majestic splendour of this well preserved Norman castle

LLANELLI
BOROUGH COUNCIL

A BETTER PLACE FOR BUSINESS & LEISURE

FOR FURTHER INFORMATION CONTACT LLANELLI BOROUGH COUNCIL, TŶ ELWYN, LLANELLI.
PHONE (0554) 742178 FAX (0554) 742140

Kidwelly

Kidwelly is an ancient town standing at the confluence of the rivers Gwendraeth Fach and Gwendraeth Fawr, which run out into the sandy Tywi estuary of Carmarthen Bay.

The town received its first charter under Henry I and is therefore one of the oldest boroughs in Wales. Indeed, many of the visitors who come here are drawn by a monument to Kidwelly's history - the medieval castle, which is remarkably well preserved and stands imposingly on a steep ridge above the river.

The town grew up around the castle and was also fortified. Though no other original town buildings survive, Kidwelly still retains something of a medieval air by virtue of the 14th-century bridge across the river and the ancient church of St. Mary the Virgin, impressive for its tall spire.

In much more recent times, Kidwelly was a busy trading port and in the 19th century was firmly established as one of Britain's largest tinplate manufacturing centres. This achievement is proudly recorded in the fascinating industrial museum, which occupies the site of the old Kidwelly Tinplate Works.

Kidwelly's fame also has a darker side. In 1920, local solicitor Harold Greenwood was accused of murdering his wife. Though he was acquitted at Carmarthen Assizes, the trial was important because it initiated the procedure of numbering the pages in police notebooks to ensure that information is accurately recorded. Greenwood lived at Capel Sul, a large house which still stands beside the bridge in Kidwelly.

ATTRACTIONS & PLACES OF INTEREST

Kidwelly Castle

The original motte and bailey castle, made of earth and timber, was built in about 1106 by Bishop Roger of Salisbury, under the sovereignty of Henry I. It was rebuilt in stone in the late 13th and early 14th centuries largely in the form in which we see it today, though there were some later medieval and Tudor additions. The castle was one of a long line of Norman fortresses which stretched west to St. Bride's Bay on the Pembrokeshire coastline. Repeatedly attacked and captured by the Welsh in its early years, the castle was strengthened by means of the concentric method of defence - building walls within walls - and is one of the finest surviving examples of this type of medieval military architecture. That much of the castle still stands today is due to the fact that it played no part in the Civil Wars, and therefore escaped the damaging attentions of Cromwell.

Kidwelly Industrial Museum

The museum was officially opened in 1988 and is the only place in Wales where you can see how tinplate was made by hand. It is situated on the banks of the Gwendraeth Fach river, on the former site of the Kidwelly Tinplate Works, which ceased production in 1941, and the 164-foot chimney stack rising high above the valley provides an unmistakeable landmark. The museum also provides an insight into the history of the local coal industry. Among the many fascinating items to be seen here are waterwheels, industrial steam and diesel locomotives, a steam crane, brickworks, hot and cold rolling mills, colliery pit-head gear, and even a typesetting machine from the local newspaper, the *Star*.

Kidwelly Quay

Here you will find one of the first canals to be built in Wales. Recently restored, it provides a superb picnic area and serves as a reminder of the days when Kidwelly was a thriving port.

St. Mary's Church

Once the church of the Benedictine Priory, it is notable for its spire, which was a later addition to the 13th-century tower. Inside the church is a 14th-century alabaster statue of the Virgin and Child.

SPORTS AND ACTIVITIES

Those in search of an active holiday will not be disappointed in this corner of Wales. Sports and recreational facilities in and around Llanelli are first-class, as the following shows. Further details are available from the Tourist Information Centres at Llanelli and Pont Abraham, which are listed on page 96.

Llanelli Leisure Centre

Located adjacent to People's Park, this superb new sports and leisure complex combines many excellent all-weather facilities under one roof. Star attractions are the Jubilee Pool, which features a hydroslide and a junior splash pool, and the Sports Hall, where aerobics, badminton, cricket, short tennis and other team games are played. A state-of-the-art fitness gym is complemented by a well-equipped health suite (with sauna and solarium), and glass-backed courts provide the perfect venue for squash and racquet ball. To recover from all this activity, you can relax in the bar and coffee shop, and the Centre even has its own purpose-built registered creche. For any further information ring 0554 756249.

Selwyn Samuel Bowls Centre, Llanelli

An indoor bowling complex for international matches and club games, as well as public use. Open from September to April, it has 6 rinks, changing facilities and a restaurant.

Pontnewydd Golf Centre

Members and visitors are equally welcome at this outstanding new golf centre, just a few miles north-west of Llanelli in the beautiful Gwendraeth Valley. The challenging 18-hole par-72 course, 6173 yards in length, was designed by one of Britain's leading golf architects. The centre's facilities, some of which are still under development at the time of going to press, include a 9-hole course, 12-bay driving range, professional shop, first-class clubhouse,tuition, competitions, and the Bryn Fforest Inn.

For more details on any of the places featured in this guide, contact the local Tourist Information Centres listed on page 96.

Brace Harvatt Associates

OTHER SPORTS FACILITIES

Aikido
Llanelli is the home of the Welsh Aikido Association, which holds an annual summer school at Burry Port. You can also participate at the YMCA, Stepney Street, Llanelli (ring 0554 774898).

Angling
*Lliedi Reservoir: permits from Welsh Water Authority (0792 468000)
*Furnace Pond, Llanelli
*Llanelli Beach
*Cefn Sidan Sands
*Boats from Burry Port (0554 832740)
*Burry Port Fishing Festival

Badminton
*Llanelli Leisure Centre
*Bryngwyn Sports Centre, Dafen, Llanelli (0554 754686)
*Coedcae Sports Centre, Llanelli (0554 770591)
*Stradey Sports Centre, Pwll Road, Llanelli (0554 772986)
*Glanymor Sports Centre, Burry Port (0554 834659)

Basketball
*Stradey Sports Centre, Pwll Road, Llanelli (0554 772986)

Bowls
*Selwyn Samuel Centre, Park Crescent, Llanelli (0554 776506)
*Burry Port Memorial Park, Burry Port (0554 834497)
*Parc Howard, Felinfoel Road, Llanelli (0554 770929)
*People's Park, Park Crescent, Llanelli
*Parc Stephens, Kidwelly (0554 891046)

Canoeing
*Pembrey Country Park
*Lliedi Reservoir
*Sandy Water Park, Llanelli (canoe hire available)
*Kidwelly Quay (canoe hire available)

Cricket
*Llanelli Cricket Club, Stradey, Llanelli (0554 773721)

Cycling
*Bike hire is available at Pembrey Country Park during summer months.

Golf
*Pontnewydd Golf Course, Trimsaran (0554 810278)
*Ashburnham Golf Club, Burry Port (0554 832269)
*Tycroes Golf Range, Tycroes (0269 596460)
*Pembrey Pitch & Putt, Pembrey Country Park (0554 833913)

Gymnasium
*YMCA, Stepney Street, Llanelli (0554 774898)

Horse Riding
*Clyn-Du Riding Centre, Pembrey Mountain (0554 832546)
*Equestrian Centre, Pembrey Country Park (0554 832160)

Karting
*Circuit Scene, Pembrey Circuit (Kart hire available. 0554 891455)

Kite Buggying
*Pembrey Country Park

Land Yachting
*Cefan Sidan Land Yacht Club (0554 832022)

Motorsports and Racing Driving
*The Welsh Motorsports Centre (racing/tuition/karting/rallying)

Multigym
*Bryngwyn Sports Centre, Dafen, Llanelli (0554 754686)
*Glanymor Sports Centre, Burry Port (0554 834659)

Netball
*Stradey Sports Centre, Pwll Road, Llanelli (0554 772986)

Orienteering
*Pembrey Country Park

Pitch & Putt
*Pembrey Country Park (0554 833913)

Rowing
*Sandy Water Park, Llanelli

Rugby
*Llanelli RFC, Stradey Park (0554 774060)

Skiing
*Pembrey Country Park (0554 834443)

Snooker
*Terry Griffiths Matchroom, Riley Snooker Club, Llanelli (0554 774494)

Squash
*Llanelli Leisure Centre
*Llanelli & District Tennis and Squash Club

Soccer
*Llanelli AFC, Stebonheath, Llanelli (0554 772973)

Swimming Pools
*Jubilee Pool, Llanelli Leisure Centre (0554 774757)

Tennis
*Llanelli Leisure Centre
*Parc Howard, Llanelli
*Llanelli & District Tennis and Squash Club

Tobogganing
*Pembrey Country Park (0554 834443)

Walking
There are many excellent trails and footpaths in the area, such as the Furnace Pond Trail and the Lower Lliedi Reservoir country walk, both of which are described in free leaflets available from the Tourist Information Centres in Llanelli and at Pont Abraham (listed on page 96). Pembrey Country Park also has nature trails and throughout the year offers a programme of guided walks.

Windsurfing
*Sandy Water Park, Llanelli (equipment hire available)
*Cefn Sidan Sands

Yachting
*Burry Port
*Sandy Water Park, Llanelli

FESTIVALS AND EVENTS

Every year a number of festivals and exhibitions are held in the Llanelli area.

Llanelli Flower Festival
A traditional event since the 1800's, and recently revived. Held early September.

Gwyl Llanelli Festival
Held in November and offering a variety of entertainment in the form of concerts, recitals, live theatre, street theatre and ballet.

Llanelli Christmas Carnival
The largest carnival in Wales, held in November. Festive floats and a spectacular firework display greet the arrival of Father Christmas in Llanelli.

Burry Port Fishing Festival
Attracts anglers from all over the UK and offers excellent prizes and entertainment.

Welsh Festival of Motorsport
High-speed, low-cost entertainment for all. A full racing programme is complemented by side shows, entertainment and displays.

Swansea Bay & Mumbles

The old adage that history repeats itself holds a certain ring of truth for Swansea. Founded by the Vikings, developed into a busy administrative and trading centre by the Normans, established as a prosperous industrial ans seaside town by the Victorians, and flattened by the bombs of the Luftwaffe, Swansea has seen the clock turn full circle. Today it again stands tall as a thriving regional capital, just as it did in the medieval period.

Now, as then, Swansea enjoys several key roles. Local pride is not slow to point out that since 1969, with the Investiture of Prince Charles as Prince of Wales, Swansea's status has been elevated to that of a city. And as a Welsh city by the sea, second only to Cardiff in size and importance, it is now a popular holiday resort, a university city, a centre for shopping, recreation, leisure and commerce, and the administrative centre for the county of West Glamorgan. It is also the birthplace of Dylan Thomas, Sir Harry Secombe and Catherine Zeta Jones.

To the many thousands of day trippers and holidaymakers who flock to the area each year, Swansea Bay, Mumbles and the Gower Peninsula provide a wholly satisfying mix of magnificent beaches and scenery, great family attractions and entertainment, first-class leisure and sports facilities, a wide choice of accommodation, and a wonderful sense of history and Welsh culture.

There can be few other places in Wales which display such a varied and colourful character as does Swansea. And by virtue of the city's ability to turn adversity into opportunity, visitors today can enjoy a veritable feast of things to see and do.

One of the best examples is the award-winning Maritime Quarter. This very impressive development occupies the former site around the old South Dock, which from its opening in 1859 was instrumental in Swansea's expansion as a major exporter of coal and copper. Now, in place of the warehouses, coal hoists and railway

Swansea Marina

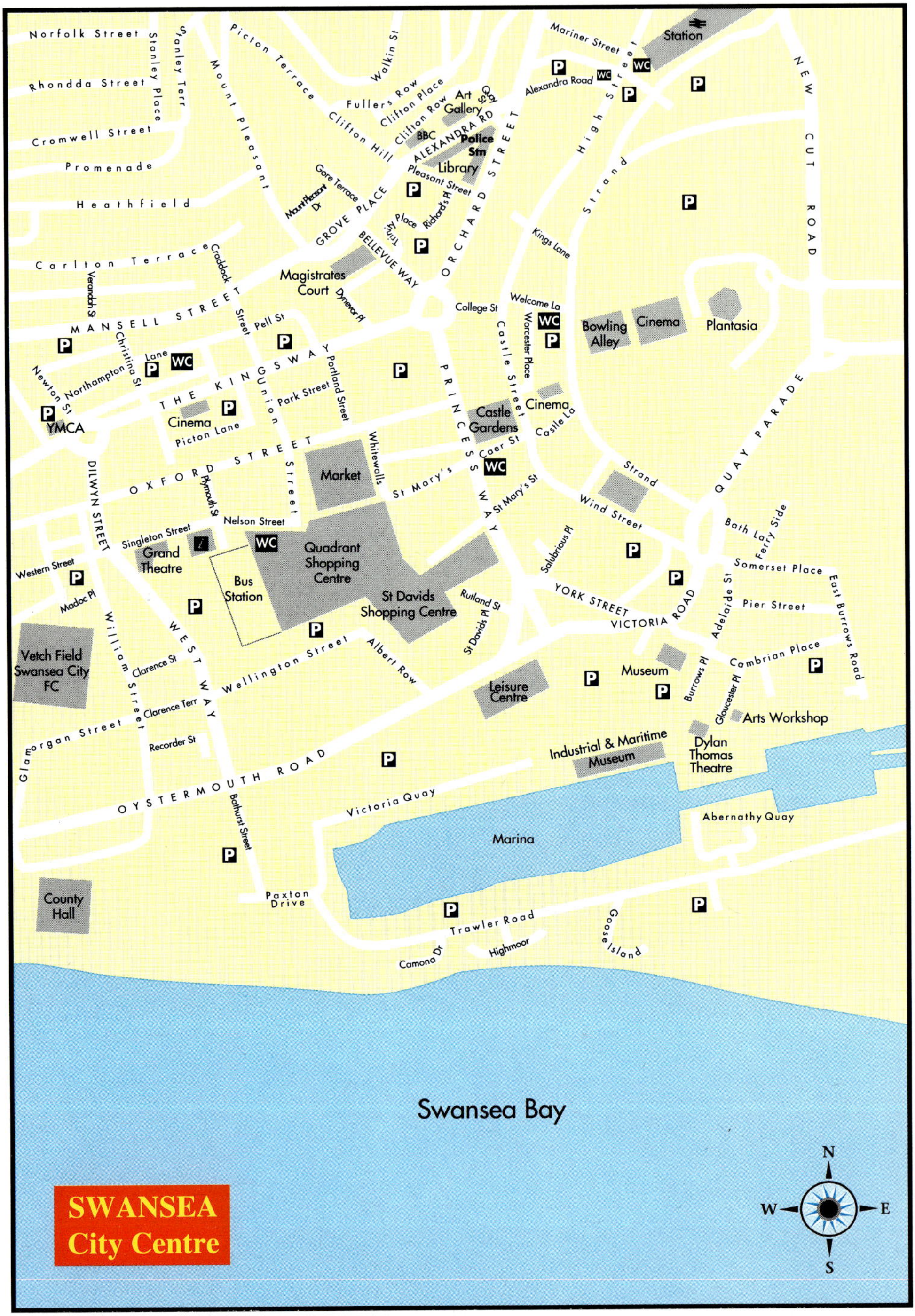
SWANSEA
City Centre
Swansea Bay
N
S
E
W
Norfolk Street
Rhondda Street
Cromwell Street
Promenade
Heathfield
Carlton Terrace
Stanley Place
Stanley Terr
Mount Pleasant
Picton Terrace
Walkin St
Fullers Row
Clifton Place
Clifton Row
Clifton Hill
Art Gallery
Quay St
BBC
ALEXANDRA RD
Police Stn
Library
Pleasant Street
Gore Terrace
Mount Pleasant Dr
GROVE PLACE
Trinity Place
Richard's Pl
BELLEVUE WAY
ORCHARD STREET
Mariner Street
Station
WC
Alexandra Road
High Street
Strand
NEW CUT ROAD
Kings Lane
Magistrates Court
Dynevor Pl
Verandah St
Craddock Street
MANSELL STREET
Pell St
College St
Welcome La
Worcester Place
Castle Street
Bowling Alley
Cinema
Plantasia
Christina St
Northampton Lane
Newton St
YMCA
THE KINGSWAY
Union Street
Park Street
Portland Street
PRINCESS WAY
Castle Gardens
Castle La
Picton Lane
OXFORD STREET
Whitewalls
Market
St Mary's
Caer St
St Mary's St
Strand
Wind Street
QUAY PARADE
DILWYN STREET
Plymouth St
Nelson Street
Singleton Street
Grand Theatre
Bus Station
Quadrant Shopping Centre
St Davids Shopping Centre
Salubrious Pl
Bath La
Ferry Side
Somerset Place
East Burrows Road
Western Street
Madoc Pl
YORK STREET
VICTORIA ROAD
Adelaide St
Pier Street
Rutland St
St Davids Pl
Albert Row
Vetch Field Swansea City FC
William Street
Clarence St
WEST WAY
Wellington Street
Leisure Centre
Museum
Burrows Pl
Gloucester Pl
Cambrian Place
Arts Workshop
Clarence Terr
Glamorgan Street
Recorder St
OYSTERMOUTH ROAD
Industrial & Maritime Museum
Dylan Thomas Theatre
Victoria Quay
Bathurst Street
Marina
Abernathy Quay
County Hall
Paxton Drive
Trawler Road
Goose Island
Camona Dr
Highmoor
P

Swansea Marina

Brace Harvatt Associates

embankments which once stood here, you will find an attractive waterfront village with a host of interesting features - shops, pubs, eating places, a theatre, craft workshops, floating exhibits, a leisure centre, museum, nightclub and more - all clustered around the 600-berth marina, just a few minutes' walk from the city centre.

In 1993 the marina was greatly enhanced and extended with the building of the £17 million River Tawe Barrage - the first tidal river barrage (as opposed to flood defence system) to be completed anywhere in Britain. This structure stretches 70 yards across the mouth of the river and its effect is to make the marina accessible to boats at virtually all stages of the tide. Another benefit of the barrage's ingenious design is production of electricity by the built-in hydro-generator, which works with the changing tides. The barrage is also good for the environment. It prevents any sea pollution from entering the Tawe and has enhanced the appearance of the riverside at low tide.

Another great attraction of Swansea is the city itself. Though most of the old town was destroyed in air raids in 1941, the excellent modern shopping facilities reflect the fact that the area's population is approaching 200,000 and is massively swollen by visitors throughout the year. A highlight not to be missed is the covered market, which though housed in a modern complex is one of the oldest markets in Wales, its traditions firmly rooted in medieval times. This is where you will find laverbread, a speciality of Swansea which is made from a particular strain of seaweed and is something of an acquired taste!

Unlike many modern cities which are all shops and traffic and very little else, Swansea has a great deal to show you - much of it steeped in Welsh culture.

The ruins of Swansea Castle stand near the city centre, one of eleven castles which bear testimony to Norman rule in the area.

There are many parks and gardens in and near the city, such as Clyne Gardens - famous for its rhododendrons and azaleas - and Cwmdonkin Park, a favourite boyhood haunt of the great Swansea poet Dylan Thomas.

Museums and galleries, displaying many treasures and works of art, include the Glynn Vivian Art Gallery, the Maritime and Industrial Museum, and Swansea Museum - the oldest in Wales.

On a more lively note, Swansea offers a variety of entertainment from the stages of the Grand Theatre and Brangwyn Hall, as well as through major events such as the Swansea Festival and Swansea Fringe. At Parc Tawe, a leisure complex east of the city, you will also find a 10-screen cinema. And there are nightclubs, restaurants, bustling city centre pubs, activities such as ten-pin bowling, and the opportunity to sample traditional Welsh fare and entertainment at the Hwyrnos - a novel experience described on page 32.

Festivals are always an important item on the city's agenda - varying from the Lord Mayor's Parade to the Christmas Market - and in 1995 Swansea becomes Britain's first ever City of Literature. This year-long celebration of the written word is part of the Art Council's Arts 2000 initiative, the aim of which is to break down prejudices and intellectual barriers and encourage participation in the arts by a much wider audience. The promise is that for the whole of 1995 Swansea will be a vibrant, exciting, non-stop festival of street theatre and major performances.

Singleton Park

Participation of a different kind can be enjoyed by visitors to the Swansea Leisure Centre, which provides a choice of sporting and leisure activities that is in every sense breathtaking. One of the very few things it lacks is a golf course - but there are many fine courses around Swansea Bay, which is also a favourite venue for watersports and fishing.

As for Swansea's many other attractions, these are described on pages 31-37. But one worthy of special mention is Plantasia. This is a £2.5 million hothouse garden which beneath its single glass roof has recreated three distinct climatic zones. In these computer-controlled conditions thrive thousands of tropical and sub-tropical plants, including species which are now extinct in the wild.

So when you have seen the sights of Swansea and feel it is time to enjoy the sea, how far do you have to go? Hardly any distance at all. Because just a few minutes from the city centre is the big smiling crescent of Swansea Bay. And that leads to another great holiday attraction...

The Mumbles

From the east, the long shoreline of Swansea Bay is interrupted by the River Tawe before curving round in a wide 5-mile sweep to its southern tip at the Mumbles.

This village resort was discovered by the Victorians and has been a popular holiday destination ever since. It has everything you expect of a typical British seaside resort. A Victorian pier (900 feet long) with its fishermen, funfair, helter skelter, amusement arcade, cafe and nightclub; a wide expanse of sand and deckchairs; a long promenade, which extends back along the bay to the east of Swansea city centre; a lighthouse, built in 1793 and Mumbles' best-known landmark; an abundance of pubs, clubs and restuarants, scattered along the famous Mumbles Mile; and an assortment of gift and other shops where you can idly browse in the evening after a hard day of holiday enjoyment.

The Mumbles even has a castle, grander than Swansea's and perched on a hill above the village of Oystermouth. It is a development of the original Oystermouth Castle, which was destroyed by the Welsh in the 13th century, and is in a remarkably good state of preservation. From this lofty position the views over the bay and Mumbles Head are spectacular.

Oystermouth is in fact a more accurate name for the settlement which has come to be known as the Mumbles, for this is the village around which the resort has grown up. The name is also a reflection of the once-thriving trade in local oysters. These days Oystermouth is a charming village of attractive streets lined with gift and craft shops, one of which has achieved no little fame by specialising in traditional Welsh wooden lovespoons.

Fame is no stranger to the Mumbles, having arrived here as early as 1804 with the opening of the Mumbles Railway to transport coal and limestone. It was horsedrawn and ran for about 5 miles from Swansea to Oystermouth. By 1807 it was also carrying up to 18 passengers and so reputedly became the world's first ever passenger railway. In 1877 the horse (hopefully not the same one) was replaced by steam, and in 1929 there was a further progression, this time to double-decker electric trams with a distinctive red livery.

The familiar sight of these trams found affection with locals and holidaymakers alike, and they were sorely missed when the service closed in 1960. One consolation, however, is that the journey can now be made along a cycle and pedestrian path which runs from Swansea Marina to Mumbles Pier. Bikes and tandems are readily available for hire.

Now a popular venue for water-skiing, windsurfing, yachting and other watersports, the Mumbles has one other ace up its sleeve. This is the gateway to Britain's first Area of Outstanding Natural Beauty - the totally unspoilt Gower Peninsula (described on pages 38-48).

From longships to pleasure boats

Many of the early settlements which grew around the coastlines of West Wales regularly fell victim to marauding Vikings, whose favourite pastime was robbing churches of their riches and torching villages and homesteads.

But as well as destroying communities, the Vikings also created them. Swansea is a case in point. The name derives from *Sweyn's ey* (meaning inlet or island) - a possible reference to Swein Forkbeard. He was King of Denmark from 986 to 1014, and it is known that he visited the Bristol Channel.

Artefacts on show in Swansea Museum prove that the Romans also occupied the area. But typically it was the Normans who brought order and prosperity, first building a castle and then developing the town of Swansea around it.

Swansea quickly became a busy centre of administration and trade. It was granted several royal charters and soon had town walls and a church, a thriving harbour, a weekly market and regular fairs. A few miles away, at Oystermouth, a second castle was built.

Much of this good work was undone by Owain Glyndwr in the period of Welsh revolt between 1400 and 1410, when the town and castle of Swansea were seized and laid to ruin.

Yet with the resilience which was to typify Swansea's character throughout its history, in time the town not only recovered but achieved a position as a major port and industrial centre. It was coal, discovered in seams close to the surface in the land around Swansea Bay, which provided this great export opportunity.

These same deposits also enabled Swansea to become one of the world's most important centres for the manufacture of metal during the 18th and 19th centuries. In 1716 a copper works was established here. The abundance of coal led to the growth of more, and by the end of the 19th century all but one of the copper works in Britain were to be found in the Swansea area.

The production of nickel, zinc, tinplate and steel developed alongside the copper industry, and

South West Wales became a centre of tinplate manufacture. By the 1890's about 75% of Britain's tinplate mills were located within 20 miles of Swansea, many of them in the Lower Swansea Valley.

This proliferation of heavy industry and collieries certainly created wealth, but it also destroyed much of the landscape of the valley. In 1960 work began in earnest on restoring it to something like its original state, and over 30 years later the Lower Swansea Valley is regarded as an excellent example of how land devastated by industrial activity and pollution **can** be reclaimed given time, effort, money and care.

While industry was doing its worst for the environment of Swansea Bay in the 19th century, the areas to the south and west of the town had aspirations on becoming a fashionable and stylish resort.

They were no doubt encouraged by the earlier success of one of Swansea's most famous sons, Richard "Beau" Nash (1674-1762). In 1704 he had become master of the ceremonies in Bath, and the flair and splendour with which he conducted public balls had not been seen before. He was also instrumental in reforming manners and social graces, influential in the improvements of streets and buildings, and a leader of fashion - all of which had helped transform Bath into a fashionable holiday centre.

Swansea had high hopes of following suit. For a time it succeeded and was frequented by ladies and gentlemen to whom the continent was out of bounds because of the territorial ambitions of a certain Napoleon Bonaparte. The attentions of high society meant that by the early 1800's Swansea town centre boasted a reputable theatre, respectable hotels, bathing facilities, and a busy programme of balls, regattas, race meetings and cricket matches. And wealthy local industrialists, such as the Vivian family, built splendid homes to the west of the town and helped enhance the impression that Swansea could indeed become another Bath.

However, the unstoppable wheels of the area's industry eventually clouded all such ambitions. In fact, Swansea's success as an industrial and maritime centre went from strength to strength,

Swansea Bay

peaking in the years that led up to the First World War. But from the top the only way was down, and in the decades which followed there was a decline in the metal industries and the town's prosperity. The once-thriving docks were suddenly dependent solely on the export of anthracite and the import of oil for the refinery at nearby Llandarcy.

Swansea was dealt a further blow in February 1941 when the medieval and Victorian heart of the old town was torn out by air raids which destroyed many fine buildings, including St. Mary's church and the market. Rebuilding proved to be a slow process, hindered by the continuing decline of the old industries.

But Swansea's refusal to lie down eventually turned things round. The steel industry was modernised and the economy began to improve. In 1969, the year in which he became Prince of Wales, Prince Charles granted Swansea the status of a city. And with the local government reorganisation of Britain in 1974, Swansea was declared the administrative centre of the new county of West Glamorgan.

Since then the emphasis has moved away from industry and on to tourism and leisure, though the city still has a strong industrial and commercial presence in the form of modern industrial estates and business parks. Shipping also makes a valuable contribution to the local economy, one of the most regular and distinctive visitors to the port being the daily Swansea-Cork passenger and car ferry.

Swansea today is a thriving and very agreeable city by the sea - the ideal base from which to discover the many pleasures of Swansea Bay and the countless treasures of beautiful South and West Wales.

ATTRACTIONS & PLACES OF INTEREST

Swansea Maritime Quarter and Marina

The rejuvenation of the old docklands has seen the creation of this award-winning Maritime Quarter. Complementing the 600-berth marina - to which boats now have virtually permanent access with the completion of the River Tawe Barrage - are attractive shops, pubs, places to eat and a variety of great attractions. These include the Industrial and Maritime Museum; Swansea Leisure Centre; a night club; Dylan Thomas Square - a focal point for marina events such as the August Sea Shanty Festival; the Dylan Thomas Theatre; craft workshops; and a gallery with exhibits of local work.

Maritime and Industrial Museum

This novel museum is designed to entertain the whole family as well as to provide information about Swansea's past. It incorporates a working woollen mill, where you can see traditional methods of dyeing, carding, spinning and weaving, and watch fleece being made into cloth exactly as it would have been over a century ago. The museum also presents historic floating exhibits, such as an ex-Gower lightship, moored alongside in the marina. A tramshed display tells the story of the Mumbles Railway - the world's first passenger railway. And in the museum's gift shop you can buy pure wool products made on site in the mill, as well as souvenirs, toys, books, cards and jewellery. Ring 0792 650351.

Plantasia

Located on the Parc Tawe complex close to the Maritime Quarter, Plantasia is a hugely impressive glass pyramid containing over 5000 plants - including more than 1000 different varieties - as well as lizards, snakes, insects, an aviary and an aquarium. Its award-winning contruction utilises 37 tons of glass to create a hothouse garden which is divided into 3 climatic zones - desert, tropical and temperate. Humidity, temperature, ventilation and light levels are computer-controlled to maintain a constant level throughout the year. Plantasia also has a souvenir shop selling plants, curios, books, gifts, and hot and cold drinks. There is full access for disabled visitors, and wheelchairs are available. Ring 0792 474555.

Glyn Vivian Art Gallery

Housed in an elegant Edwardian building in the city centre, this gallery was declared the best museum of fine and applied art in the 1992 National Heritage Awards. The permanent collections on display include fine examples of rare and richly-decorated Swansea Porcelain, as well as works of 19th-century maritime painters and distinguished local artist Ceri Richards. Also on show are European and Oriental ceramics, clocks and paperweights. Touring exhibitions are another regular feature. The Gallery Shop offers prints, pots, unusual jewellery, cards, books and other original gift ideas. Admission to the gallery is free. Ring 0792 655006.

Swansea Museum

Established in 1841, this is the oldest museum in Wales and it occupies a classically-styled 19th-century building with an imposing colonnaded entrance. The fascinating items on display range from local archaeological finds to treasures from ancient Egypt. There are examples of 19th-century costume, Victorian collections of natural history, a collection of Swansea and Nantgarw porcelain and pottery, and a history trail of the Lower Swansea Valley. Admission to the museum is free. Ring 0792 653763.

Swansea Market

Swansea has been well known for its markets since medieval times, when they were held in the streets around the castle. A new market hall was built in the 1890's and was the pride of the town until it was badly damaged during the 1941 air raids. The market is now located in the Quadrant Shopping Centre, yet still retains much of its old character and traditions. On offer is an excellent choice of fresh fish, seafood, local farm produce ranging from Welsh lamb to vegetables, and specialities such as cockles - fresh from the beds at nearby Penclawdd - and laverbread.

Grand Theatre

Here you can enjoy the very best in live entertainment - Shakespeare to musicals, opera to comedy, ballet to children's shows. For details of booking and current programme ring 0792 475715.

Brangwyn Hall

This is the city's principal concert hall, offering

Swansea Market

performances by the world's finest orchestras, soloists and conductors. It is located within Swansea Guildhall and is named after the Brangwyn Panels, or British Empire Panels as they are also known. This stunning series of murals, based on the theme of the British Empire, was commissioned by the House of Lords and painted by Sir Frank Brangwyn in the 1920's and '30's. But the Lords rejected them because they considered the panels too bright and vivid - presumably on the grounds that such a shocking display of colour might distract some members from dropping off during parliamentary debate.

Hwyrnos

If the promise of a traditional Welsh evening out is to your liking, this is the venue for you. A veritable feast of food, music and fun includes music and song of Wales, the Welsh harp, Welsh clog dancing, and generous portions of cawl, roast lamb, home-made apple souffle, and a litre of wine between every six guests. Vegetarian dishes are available by prior arrangement. Most of the spoken language is English, but visitors of any nationality are guaranteed an enjoyable night out whether they understand the language or not! This is also your opportunity to acquire the unique Hwyrnos Certificate of Competence in the Welsh Clog Dance. Children are welcome. Advance booking is strongly recommended by ringing 0792 641437 or any Tourist Information Centre.

Taliesin Arts Centre

Situated in Swansea University, this modern arts centre has a fully-equipped theatre, a cinema and an art gallery, as well as a bank and bookshop. For details of events ring 0792 296883.

The Craft Workshops & Pottery

A collection of artist and craft studios which includes silk painting, spinning, weaving, knitwear, pottery, soft furnishings, porcelain modelling, coopering and fine art. Finished work for sale is on display. Tuition is also available. Ring 0792 653871.

Swansea Arts Workshop Gallery

Located in the Maritime Quarter, this unique artist-run gallery has an exhibition gallery focusing on contemporary art and craft from Wales, Britain and abroad. On sale are original ceramics, jewellery, prints and cards. Ring 0792 652016.

Attic Gallery

One of Wales' leading privately-run galleries, which since 1962 has represented the work of established contemporary artists. There is a changing display of paintings, original prints and sculpture, and a regular programme of exhibitions. Ring 0792 653387.

The Lovespoon Gallery

The Mumbles' unique gallery, dedicated entirely to Welsh lovespoons and containing examples of spoons carved by more than 30 individual carvers from all over Wales. Ring 0792 360132.

Clyne Farm Activity Centre

Highly experienced instructors offer a varied programme of activitity holidays and courses, ranging from half a day to a week. Horseriding, canoeing, craft workshops, abseiling and caving are among the subjects covered. Other facilities include an assault course, archery, camping and an indoor climbing wall. Ring 0792 403333.

Swansea Laser Quest

The ultimate sci-fi adventure game. Special effects, lighting, smoke and chilling music add to the drama and excitement of Laserdome. Other facilities here include a video arcade. Ring 0792 653433.

Clyne Gardens

Open since 1953, these magnificent gardens were formerly the home of the Vivian family and are famous for their azaleas and rhododendrons. The 50 acres are divided into different types of garden, together displaying a fascinating variety of specimens collected from all over the world. There is even a wildflower meadow. In May the gardens attract thousands of visitors with the spectacularly colourful event known as Clyne in Bloom.

Clyne Valley Country Park

Adjacent to Clyne Gardens, about 4 miles west of the city centre, this is Swansea's only country park. The 700 acres provide major recreational opportunities for locals and visitors alike, and attractions here currently include an outdoor pursuits centre, a cycle path which runs along the route of the old LMS railway track bed, an adventure park, picnic areas, and woodland walks. Development of the park is still in progress, the overall aim being to conserve and manage the Clyne Valley's natural beauty and to create greater awareness of its important industrial heritage and archaeology. The park is well worth a visit whether you explore it on foot, bike or horesback.

Singleton Park

A large and attractive park of rolling grasslands and woodland which is the venue for the annual City of Swansea Show and other summer events. It has botanical gardens, a boating lake, crazy golf, a children's play area, a cafe and pub.

Brynmill Park

An ideal park for children, with a duck-filled lake, pets' corner and a playground. This is Swansea's oldest surviving park, dating from the middle of the 19th century.

Cwmdonkin Park

Dylan Thomas was born at 5 Cwmdonkin Drive, a semi in the Uplands district of Swansea, in 1914. As a boy this park was one of his favourite haunts, and the memory of it merited several mentions in his poetry and prose. The park fondly remembers Dylan too, in the form of a memorial stone inscribed with lines from *Fern Hill,* one of his best-known poems.

St, Mary's Church

The medieval church of Swansea, founded in the 12th century. Badly damaged by bombs in the Second World War, it was rebuilt for the third time in 1955. The previous two occasions were in 1745 and 1898.

Oystermouth Castle

Enjoying panoramic views over Swansea Bay and the Mumbles, the substantial remains of 13th-century Oystermouth Castle are in exceptionally good condition. It was built by the de Breos family, who ruled Gower until the 1320's, and it replaced the original 12th-century castle which had been destroyed by the Welsh. Designed more as a mansion than a fortress, it has many interesting features, including an elegant chapel window in the south-east tower.

Crymlyn Bog National Nature Reserve

The reserve is located at Bonymaen, just a mile north-east of Swansea city centre, and it affords a rare opportunity to view a wealth of plants, insects and birds in an unspoilt environment. The Visitor Centre has photographic displays of the species found here, and an illustrated history. An easy circular route has been established to take you along the edge of the bog, and other areas are accessible only with the warden's permission. The bog is managed by the Countryside Council for Wales and has free parking and a picnic area. Groups are welcome but it is essential to contact the warden first. For more information ring 0792 459255.

FESTIVALS AND EVENTS

Swansea holds an extensive and varied programme of events throughout the year, including the Lord Mayor's Parade, City of Swansea Show, Vintage Car Rally, Sea Shanty Festival, outdoor opera in the setting of Oystermouth Castle, Pontardawe Folk Festival, Radio One Roadshow, Swansea Market Cockle Festival, Swansea Music Festival, Swansea Festival and Swansea Fringe, Bonfire Night Firework Display, and the Christmas Market. For dates and current information ring or visit any Tourist Information Centre listed on page 96.

SPORTS & ACTIVITIES

Whatever your sporting interest, you will find it well catered for within the area of Swansea Bay and Gower. Here is a guide to some of the many sports, leisure and recreational facilities available here.

Swansea Leisure Centre

Already a big attraction, Swansea Leisure Centre has improved its facilities still further and offers something for everyone in the family.

The leisure pool, for example, is one of the biggest and best-equipped pools in Wales, with interactive animals in the toddlers' pool, hydroslide and aquecatch, space bowl, water slides, waves and even a beach!

The Jolly Roger is one of the largest children's soft play areas in the country, featuring such attractions as bouncy castles, inflatable ball ponds and much more to delight all children up to about 9 years old - and it opens every day of the school holidays and every weekend.

The Fun Club provides an action-packed programme of activities - from team games, racquet sports and swimming to arts, crafts and much more - for children up to 13.

Fitkid is a new programme of wacky warm-ups, crazy circuits, spacehoppers, parachutes and other mad-cap fun to exercise body and mind of all youngsters aged 5 to 13. There are awards for attendance, prizes to be won and the Fitkid Club, which offers many other benefits.

Swansea Leisure Centre has a great deal for adults too - particularly in the area of health and fitness, where the stated aim of the programmes and classes is to engender a total feeling of well being in participants.

First there's a choice of health and fitness classes, available at the Leisure Centre throughout the week. They range from STEP and aerobics to circuit training and ladies' keep fit, and all classes can be booked in advance.

Then there is the newly-extended Workhouse Fitness Centre, which looks well equipped to help you along the way. Its sophisticated new cardio-vascular equipment includes cycles which read your pulse and automatically adjust pedal resistance; stepping machines which have proven to be highly effective fat-burning and aerobic exercises; jogging machines which can be programmed to simulate different speeds and gradients; and a machine called the Versa-Climber, which is described as presenting the ultimate aerobic challenge. The Workhouse now also provides more space for free weights, which are an important part of any exercise programme. And to make sure that you really reap the benefit of the energy you expend in the Workhouse, the Leisure Centre's qualified staff can design a personal exercise programme just for you.

In contrast, the Neptune Health Suite is much more relaxing, designed to ease the pressures of everyday life. It has two spa pools, four RUVA sunbeds, steam and sauna rooms, and a changing and relaxation area.

In fact, nobody's health and fitness needs are overlooked at Swansea Leisure Centre. Fifty Plus and Ladies Exercise Plus are two other programmes available, the former comprising racquet sports, table tennis, swimming, yoga, dancing, specialist fitness sessions and more. Ladies Exercise Plus gives you the chance to swim and play racquet sports, and to join in aerobics, STEP, and circuit training - provided, of course, that you are female. For this programme a creche

is provided.

Other health and fitness initiatives at Swansea Leisure Centre include Lunch Bunch - which for one price gives you the use of squash courts, badminton courts, the Neptune Health Suite and the Workhouse Fitness Centre between mid-day and 2.00pm; Fitness and Fun - 2-hour sessions, with creche, on selected afternoons for aerobics, STEP, circuits and the Workhouse Fitness Centre; and Saturday Night Fun - 4 hours of fun for all the family, with full use of badminton and squash courts, table tennis, short tennis, swimming, Jolly Roger for the under 9's, Neptune Health Suite and the Workhouse Fitness Centre, all for one price.

For further information about Swansea Leisure Centre, ring 0792 649126 or 649121.

Morfa Stadium

A multi-purpose sports complex offering a variety of leisure opportunities, including hospitality suites catering for major sporting events and corporate challenges. Swansea City Tennis Centre, with indoor and outdoor courts, is adjacent. Ring 0792 476578.

Bowling: GXsuperbowl

A ten-pin bowling centre with 26 fully-computerised lanes, a restaurant and a licensed bar. It also has facilities for disabled visitors. It is located at Parc Tawe, next to Plantasia. Special buffet-and-bowl packages are available, and children's birthday parties are catered for. Lanes can be reserved by 'phone. Ring 0792 467364.

Cricket

The St. Helen's Ground is the home of Swansea Cricket Club, and Glamorgan's county side also make occasional appearances here. For fixtures and other information ring 0792 464918.

Cycling: Swansea Bikepath

This is part of the ambitious and exciting scheme to create a long-distance route for walkers and cyclists from Newport to Swansea, using disused railway lines and forestry tracks above the South Wales valleys. The Swansea Bikepath is the city's contribution to the project, and is being developed in sections, some of which - such as Tawe Riverside Path - are now open. When complete it will offer a tremendous variety of scenery and locations, passing for example through the Maritime Quarter, the seafront promenade, parkland, forest and open hillsides, so giving stunning views of Swansea Bay. Cycle hire is available at several places in the area. For details, and up-to-date information on the path's progress, ring Swansea City Council's Planning Department on 0792 301301.

Fishing

Sea fishing is a major sport within Swansea Bay, which incorporates some of the best angling grounds off the British coast. It is also very popular from Mumbles Pier. Boats with skippers who know the most productive areas are for hire. Cod, bass, monkfish (rock salmon) and mackarel are among the most common catches.

Karting: Supertrax Indoor Go Kart Centre

A purpose-built indoor circuit offering all the thrills and spills of grand prix racing. The centre is open throughout the year. Ring 0792 775544.

Rugby

The All Whites - Swansea Rugby Football Club - is based at the St. Helen's Ground, which it shares with Swansea Cricket Club. For rugby fixtures and information ring 0792 642381.

Skiing: Swansea Ski Centre

Located at the regional sports centre in Morfa, this dry ski slope has a separate nursery area and 2 lifts, and offers lessons for children and beginners. It is open throughout the year. Ring 0792 645639 or 367321.

Soccer

You can watch Second Divisin football at the Vetch Field, home of the Swans - Swansea City Football Club. For fixture and other details ring 0792 462584.

Look for our other guides in this series!

The Gower Peninsula

Although joined at the hip to Swansea, and officially under the city council's control since 1974, the Gower Peninsula is to all intents and purposes an island - an area virtually untouched by development and a world apart from the industrial and urban spread of South Wales.

Gower is remarkable in many respects. Designated Britain's first Area of Outstanding Natural Beauty, in 1956, the peninsula measures approximately 14 miles from east to west and about half that distance across. Within these narrow shores you can explore a great diversity of landscape: cliffs towering above golden beaches and rocky coves; hilltops commanding spectacular views over Welsh and English coastlines; open downs and wide commons leading to vast areas of saltmarsh and sand dunes.

This gloriously unspoilt scene is further enhanced by deep wooded valleys and the ruins of medieval castles and ancient burial sites. There are attractions natural and man-made, and something new to discover at every turn. Yet even the peninsula's most westerly beach, Rhossili, is within easy driving distance of the shops and amenities of Swansea's bustling city centre - a startling contrast to Gower, which does not have a single town to its name.

One of the many striking features of Gower is the difference between the northern and southern coastlines. The former is a wild estuarine landscape of saltmarsh and mudflats, for the most part devoid of human activity. Yet in the south the picture is of magnificent sandy beaches, secluded bays and dramatic headlands - a holiday paradise for families, fishermen and watersports enthusiasts.

Separating north from south is the ridge of hills known as Cefn Bryn. The views from here are tremendous, looking one way over the Loughor estuary to Carmarthenshire and the other towards Three Cliffs Bay and the Bristol Channel. Ancient ancestors evidently appreciated this perspective too, for on Cefn Bryn stands the giant cromlech called Arthur's Stone - a Neolithic burial chamber which has a 25-ton capstone.

Inevitably, Gower's magnetic attraction can result in traffic congestion at the height of summer, while some of the more remote beaches are not accessible by road at any time. But this should not worry the true explorer, for the peninsula is best seen on foot, bike or horseback. You can walk almost the entire coastline, and an exhilarating cliff path runs from Mumbles along the south coast to Worms Head - just one of the many delights awaiting you in this beautifully unspoilt corner of South Wales.

Horse at Worms Head

THE NORTH COAST

Gower's north coast is dominated by Llanrhidian Marsh - 6 miles of saltmarsh adjoining the mudflats and sandbanks of the Loughor estuary, and home to grazing sheep and wild ponies.

The marsh also attracts a great variety of birds. These include wildfowl and shellduck, and huge numbers of waders such as oystercatchers, plovers and redshanks which flock here in winter months to feed on the rich pickings of the tidal mudflats.

The estuary is a designated Ramsar site, which means it is a protected wetland conservation area of international importance. This is not its only role. Some of the biggest cockle beds in Wales are to be found here, and for generations cockle gathering was an important local industry on this part of Gower.

To the west of Llanrhidian Marsh lies the 3-mile promontory of Whiteford Burrows and Whiteford Sands, where there is a National Nature Reserve. At the northern end of the sands is Whiteford Point.

Just off the point stands a disused cast-iron lighthouse which was built in 1865 and decommissioned in 1933. Its function is now performed by an automatic light on the island of Burry Holms, situated between the bays of Broughton and Rhossili, 4 miles to the south-west.

THE WEST COAST

Gower's west coast is blessed with one of the finest beaches in Britain - Rhossili. It is overlooked by Rhossili Down, which at 634 feet is the highest hill on the peninsula. Archaeologists have literally had a field day here, as many ritual and burial sites dating from the Bronze Age have been discovered around the top of the Down.

Near the crest there are also the remains of two ancient burial chambers known as Sweyne's Howes. By tradition these are associated with the Viking warlord Sweyne - allegedly the founder of the community which developed into the city of Swansea - but they are actually Neolithic, between 4,000 and 5,500 years old.

On a clear day Rhossili Down gives panoramic views over Gower and South Pembrokeshire, and across the Bristol Channel to Somerset, Devon

Llanrhidian

and Lundy Island. The Down also provides one of Gower's best walks, from Rhossili village to Hillend.

Below the Down is the magnificent sweep of Rhossili Bay - 3 miles of clean golden sand frequented by fishermen, surfers and hang gliders. Towards the southern end of this wonderful beach are the sad, decaying remains of the barque *Helvetia*, which was blown ashore one night in November, 1887. Behind the beach are the dunes which hide the lost village of old Rhossili, a community engulfed by the sand. The church of the present-day village has a memorial to Edgar Evans, who died with Scott in the Antarctic in 1912.

At the southern tip of Rhossili Bay, the serpent-like peninsula of Worms Head extends west for a mile into the sea. For a short period either side of low tide you can walk across it, but there are restrictions on access during the bird-nesting season, as the site is the South Gower Coast National Nature Reserve, managed by the Countryside Council for Wales.

Rhossili also has another attraction - the

Gors-las
Penygroes
A48
B4306
A484
Pontantwn
Cross Hands
A474
Llandefaelog
B4317
Capel
Hendre
AMMANF
Tumble
Pontyberem
B4309
A483
Pontyates
Llan-non
S
49
KIDWELLY
Sylen
Carway
B4306
A476
B4306
Hendy
Pontarddulais
Five Roads
48
A484
Felinfoel
BURRY PORT
M4
A48
B4297
B4489
Clydac
Pembrey
Pwll
Llwynhendy
47
46
LLANELLI
A484
Loughor
GORSEINON
Morriston
Whitford Point
B4295
A483
A4067
Penclawdd
Gowerton
Broughton
Bay
Llanmorlais
Dunvant
Llanmadoc
A4216
Three Crosses
Cheriton
Killay
SW
Llangennith
Llanrhidian
B4271
A4067
Rhosilli
Bay
Black Pill
Reynoldston
Llandewi
A4118
Knelston
Pennard
The Mumbles
Worms
Head
Penmaen
Newton
Rhossili
Mumbles Head
Oxwich
Oxwich
Bay
Port Eynon
N
W
E
S
BRISTOL

Brynamman
A4068
Abercraf
A4067
A4221
Ystradfellte
A4059
ORD
A474
Ystradgynlais
Ystalyfera
Seven Sisters
Penderyn
A4109
Hirwaun
A465
Pontardawe
Rhos
Crynant
A4067
A474
Resolven
A4061
B4291
Aberdulais
B4434
GLYNCORRWG
TREHERBERT
Tonna
45
44
NEATH
Blaengwynfi
TREORCHY
A4217
43
B4287
A4107
A48
Duffryn
Ystrad
A483
Briton Ferry
SWANSEA
Baglan
42
Cwmafan
Bryn
B4282
A4064
41
Garth
MAESTEG
PORT TALBOT
40
Taibach
A4093
SWANSEA
BAY
Ogmore
Vale
Margam
39
38
A4063
Betws
A48
A4061
Tondu
Kenfig
Hill
B4281
Aberkenfig
Sarn
B4280
S
36
M4
Pyle
Kenfig
37
BRIDGEND
Tythegston
A4106
Nottage
Merthyr
Mawr
PORTHCAWL
Ogmore
B4265
Ogmore-
by-Sea
B4524
St Bride's
Major
CHANNEL
Southerndown

Port-Eynon

National Trust Visitor Centre and shop, which is housed in two former coastguard cottages.

THE SOUTH COAST

The limestone cliffs of Gower's very popular south coast are punctured by caves in which remains of early man and animals have been discovered. The finds are proof that the mammoth, cave bear, reindeer and woolly rhinoceros have all used these caves for shelter in the distant past.

The best-known cave is Paviland, which is east of Thurba Head and famous for the so-called Red Lady of Paviland. This was a headless skeleton stained with red ochre, discovered in 1823 and thought to be that of a woman from the Roman period. Later tests and carbon dating proved it to be that of a young man who lived about 24,000 years ago. The skeleton is now in the University Museum, Oxford.

The most unusual cave is Culver Hole, near Port-Eynon - a sea cave which poses a mystery still unsolved to this day. The entrance of the cave has been almost entirely blocked by a strong

John F Hendy

Port-Eynon Church

masonry wall which rises to a height of four storeys, each marked by a "window"; the windows are connected on the inside by a flight of stone steps. The purpose of this bizarre structure is completely unknown, though the theories proposed have linked it variously with the lost castle of Port-Eynon, a home for pigeons and a hideout for smugglers.

Another interesting cave is Minchin Hole, which is east of Three Cliffs Bay and south of the village of Southgate. It is the largest bone cave on Gower, and excavations have revealed three hearths, cooking pots, bone spoons, combs, bronze brooches and spindle whorls, suggesting occupation during Iron Age and Roman periods. The animal bones found here include those of the woolly mammoth, woolly rhinoceros, narrow-nosed rhinoceros, elephant, lion and hyena.

East of Minchin Hole, just west of Pwll Du Head, is Bacon Hole. Rhinoceros and elephant bones have also been found in this cave, along with later mammals such as the wild ox, wolf and red deer.

However, it is the beaches of Gower's south coast which rank as its star attraction. They are sandy, unspoilt and almost totally uncommercialised, and some of the most secluded and appealing beaches are not very accessible, as described on pages 6-9.

Gower's beaches also offer great variety. For example, at the Mumbles (eastern) end of the south coast are the small but popular coves of Bracelet Bay and Limeslade Bay, while the bays of Rotherslade, Langland and Caswell are larger family beaches, also well patronised.

Further west, Three Cliffs Bay is one of the most picturesque on the Gower Peninsula, overlooked by the ruins of Pennard Castle and separated from the hugely popular Oxwich Bay by the headland of Great Tor.

Then there is pretty Port-Eynon, with its whitewashed cottages, excellent facilities and large sandy beach, currently the proud holder of a Premier Rural Beach Award from the Tidy Britain Group. Before the arrival of tourists, Port-Eynon was busily engaged in oyster fishing, limestone quarrying, lobstering and crabbing. It also enjoyed notoriety for another activity - smuggling. So prevalent was smuggling along this coastline that at one time no fewer than 8 excise men were stationed in this one small village!

The most westerly beach of Gower's south coast is Mewslade Bay. Secluded, isolated and sandy, it is set between Thurba Head and Tears Point, amongst magnificent cliff scenery.

A guide to all of Gower's many beaches is given on pages 6-10.

GUARDIANS OF GOWER

Such an abundance of natural beauty attracting visitors in ever-increasing numbers is bound to fuel fears that areas such as the Gower Peninsula cannot remain undeveloped and unspoilt for much longer. Hopefully these fears are unfounded, because Gower at least enjoys protection in many ways.

Ten per cent of the peninsula is owned and managed by the National Trust, who also own a large proportion of the coastline. The work of the Trust is complemented by the untiring efforts of the Gower Society.

Then there are official designations by the Countryside Council for Wales, and other authorities, of sites recognised to be of environmental and landscape importance. On Gower these include 3 National Nature Reserves, a Local Nature Reserve, a Ramsar Site (wetland of international importance), more than a dozen Sites of Special Scientific Interest (SSSI), a Special Protection Area, and 34 miles of Heritage Coast.

Pennard Castle

And since 1956 the Gower Peninsula has also enjoyed distinction as Britain's very first Area of Outstanding Natural Beauty. This designation alone protects Gower from major development, and is aimed at conserving the landscape and its wildlife while encouraging people to enjoy the area without damaging it.

But even all this is not the complete story of the concerted efforts being made to preserve Gower's natural beauty.

Swansea City Council, supported by the Countryside Council for Wales, has established the Gower Countryside Service. This works closely with visitors, local communities, farmers and landowners, and between April and September operates a full programme of special events. These range from guided walks to the pursuit of bats to a week's experience of drystone walling with the National Trust, and everyone is welcome. For details of the current programme ring the Gower Countryside Service on 0792 302741.

ATTRACTIONS & PLACES OF INTEREST

Weobley Castle

This is a fortified manor house rather than a full-blown Norman stronghold. It is perched above the Llanrhidian marshes of the Gower's northern coastline, with beautiful views across the marshland and Loughor estuary. The castle was built in the late 13th century. In 1406 it suffered damage at the hands of Owain Glyndwr during the great Welsh revolt. The castle, now in the care of Cadw (Welsh Historic Monuments), houses an exhibition on local history and the history of the castle. Ring 0792 390012.

Small World Pony Centre, Llanrhidian

This novel and interesting visitor attraction is the home of miniature ponies and other animals which represent the smallest of their breed, including sheep, pigs and pygmy goats. There is plenty here to see and do: an undercover animal nursery, small animal pens, indoor and outdoor play areas, bouncy castles, trout fishing, farm walks, go-karting, pony rides, a cafe and a souvenir shop. The centre caters for educational

Mumbles from Oystermouth Castle

visits and also sells activity toys and play equipment - swings, climbing frames and trampolines. Ring 0792 390995.

Bishop's Wood Countryside Centre and Local Nature Reserve

Adjacent to Caswell Bay beach, the Bishop's Wood reserve is 46 acres of woodland and grassland, owned and managed by Swansea City Council. There are various short nature trails through the reserve. There is also a small Visitor Centre, which has interesting displays and information about Bishop's Wood and its wildlife. Ring 0792 361703.

National Trust Visitor Centre, Rhossili

The ideal starting point from which to explore and enjoy this beautiful area. An exhibition illustrates Rhossili life and gives an insight into the National Trust's conservation work. There is also a shop selling National Trust books and other merchandise. Ring 0792 390707.

Y Felin Ddwr Mill & Craft Centre, Parkmill

This 14th-century water mill and working craftshops, based around an old farm complex, is a rare example of how country skills and trades were often practised together in rural Wales. The waterwheel and corn-grinding machinery are intact, and the workshops are used by a variety of craftspeople - including potters, painters and wooden toy makers - whose individual creations are for sale on site. The centre is open all year round, with parking, refreshments, a picnic area and access for disabled visitors. Ring 0792 371206.

Above Rhossili Bay

John F Hendy

Vale of Neath

The beautiful Vale of Neath today typifies the changing face of the South Wales valleys. The decline of the coal industry, bad for employment and the local economy but good for the landscape, saw the last of the area's deep mines close in 1990. Coal tips and industrial dereliction have already been swept away by the new broom of land reclamation, and from the revitalised town of Neath itself to the upper reaches of the Nedd and Dulais rivers, the borough of Neath is attracting a new generation of visitors in ever-growing numbers.

There is plenty for them to see. At its northern end, in the foothills of the Brecon Beacons National Park, the Vale of Neath is famous for the number and variety of its spectacular waterfalls - unique in Britain and much admired for more than two centuries by a succession of artists, poets, writers, photographers and film makers. Then there are the man-made attractions of Penscynor Wildlife Park, Gunsmoke Cowboy Town, Cefn Coed Colliery Museum, the National Trust project at Aberdulais Falls, and boat trips along the restored Neath Canal. There are also country parks and historic sites, and enough sports and activities to satisfy even the most energetic visitor.

And in 1994 the Vale of Neath will boast one very special extra attraction - the Royal National Eisteddfod of Wales. This great annual celebration of music and poetry is at the heart of Welsh culture, and the colour and pagentry of the ceremonies and traditional costume make it an enjoyable spectacle for everyone, regardless of nationality.

New-look Neath

The town of Neath, which lies at the southern end of the borough near the shoreline of Swansea Bay, was founded in the Middle Ages and has the ruins of both an ancient castle and an abbey to prove it.

Yet the town centre is virtually brand new - the product of a recent £25 million urban regeneration scheme, which included restoration of a four-mile stretch of the Neath Canal.

Aberdulais Falls

Wales Tourist Board

Neath's attractive new centre is fully pedestrianised and landscaped, with more than a hint of Victoriana. The neat rows of shops, which include some of the best-known names in the High Street, are in stark contrast to the hustle and bustle of the 19th-century covered market, where fresh local produce and Welsh fare such as laverbread and faggots and peas are always in keen demand.

The traditionally-styled Victoria Gardens recapture the spirit of a more dignified age and are a breath of fresh air. Behind the main shopping centre, housed in a Grade II listed building that stands in a conservation area, is Neath Borough Museum.

Keeping a watchful eye over the whole scene is all that remains of Neath Castle. Built in 1284, it is currently under restoration.

A lightning tour through history

The landscaped town centre and the rise of smart modern industrial units has transformed the face of the borough of Neath, which today supports a population of about 65,000.

Predictably, but no less interestingly, the area has a long history. Habitation by Bronze Age man, Iron Age man, Celts and Romans is evident at various sites throughout the borough. For example, traces of Celtic defensive hillforts can be seen at Buarch-y-Gaer and Warren Hill; Iron Age and Roman bronze objects, including tankard handles, have been found at Nant-y-Cafn brook, Seven Sisters; and the Romans, who occupied Wales for three hundred years, established the fort of Nidum to the west of Neath, the site of which is still visible on the edge of a residential area called Roman Way. The existence of Nidum had been known for a long time, but its exact location was not discovered until 1948, when building work for a new housing estate revealed it.

The Romans also established marching camps in the Neath area, along with Sarn Helen - one of the principal Roman roads in Wales, linking forts at Neath, Coelbren and Brecon.

But it was the Normans who first designated Neath as a borough. Along with castles, boroughs were intended as a means of keeping the hostile Welsh natives in check. Neath's first castle was of the motte and bailey type, and its remains were discovered near Neath Abbey, on the site of what

Wales Tourist Board

Ystradfellte Falls

Tonna

Wales Tourist Board

is currently a cement works. Neath Abbey itself, a Cistercian monastery, was founded in 1147.

A stone castle replaced the earlier one in the early 13th century. Rebellious Welsh forces attacked both the castle and the town on several occasions over the next one hundred years or so, and in the 14th century the town was hit by a succession of medieval plagues. Then came Owain Glyndwr, who in the early 15th century led a last desperate struggle to return Wales to the Welsh, and succeeded only in wreaking further devastation.

Towards the end of the medieval period the castle lost its role as the town's administrative centre, with the building of a town hall on the site of an old prison.

What remains of Neath Castle today is owned by the town's Community Council. To them has fallen the task of carrying out an extensive restoration programme.

Revolution of the industrial kind

The Vale of Neath's contribution to the industrial wealth of South Wales over the last two hundred years or so has been significant.

In fact, the area's industrial beginnings go back much further. In 1584, one of the first copper smelters to be built in Wales was established at Aberdulais Falls.

The local mining of ironstone also saw ironmaking develop in a big way, with charcoal used for smelting before the inevitable switch to coal. Eventually ore was imported from Cornwall and shipped up the River Nedd as far as Aberdulais, and the movement of ore and iron products, and the problems it created, led to the development of two canals. The Neath Canal opened in 1795 and the Tennant Canal in 1824, the latter giving a vital direct link with the docks at Swansea.

By the early 1800's the Melin-y-Cwrt Ironworks, just south of Resolven, was in production, followed in 1842 by the Venallt Ironworks. The trade in ores from Cornwall also attracted a group of Quaker industrialists, who established an ironworks at Neath Abbey, the proximity of which to coal and iron made it an

Mike Collier

ideal site. The works here produced a range of high-quality products, but the Quakers' religious principles absolutely forbade the manufacture of armament in any shape or size.

Neath's importance as a port declined with the advent of large cargo ships. But this was to the advantage of neighbouring Briton Ferry, which rapidly grew in stature as an industrial port.

In 1851 came another major change - the arrival of the railways in the Vale of Neath. They were carried here by some of Brunel's most magnificent viaducts, such as that at Pontwalby, and other architectural achievements of note in the Neath area came in the shape of elegant mansions built for wealthy industrialists. These included Rheola House, which is one of only four John Nash-designed mansions still surviving in Wales.

As the 20th century approached, the ironworks and coal mines continued to create the area's industrial wealth. Another local product was gunpowder, manufactured just north of Glynneath until 1940.

The South Wales' coal industry reached its peak in 1913. Production was at record levels and there were more pits open than at any other time. The picture today could hardly be more different. The last of the deep mines closed at Blaennant in 1990, and though there is still opencast mining and a number of small private mines in the upper Neath and Dulais valleys, the great days of coal are clearly over.

Neath still has its share of industry - including several multi-national companies - these days located above ground in modern purpopse-built factories, units and industrial estates. But the industry of most interest to visitors is tourism. And with so much on offer in the Vale of Neath, it's an industry already taking off in a big way.

Neath's hall of fame

The Neath area has strong connections with several well-known names, particularly eminent Victorians. Tregelles Price, for example, was a leading Quaker industrialist who became a social reformer of international repute, dedicated to the abolition of slavery and capital punishment. He also founded the Peace Society.

William Weston Young (1776-1847), another Quaker, owned a brickworks at Pontwalby, Glynneath. He developed the Dinas firebrick - a product of exceptional quality, made from silica, which became known all over Europe and America because of its ability to withstand very high temperatures. It was used to line iron and steel furnaces, lime kilns and domestic fieplaces until the works closed in 1920. The silica to make

Gwydion Roberts

the bricks was mined locally, an industry which thrived from the early 1820's to the early part of this century. William Weston Young was also a talented writer and artist. He wrote the very first guide book to the Vale of Neath, and painted the area's landscapes and natural history.

Another man to study the natural history of the Neath area was the eminent Victorian biologist Alfred Russell Wallace (1823-1918). It was he who coined the phrase "natural selection", having developed the theory of evolution quite independently of Darwin. However, they did work together and in 1858 presented a joint paper on the subject to the Linnean Society.

South Wales attracted many wealthy travellers in the 18th and 19th centuries, a number of whom were inspired to paint the wonderful landscapes they found here. Thomas Horner painted a series of watercolours of the Vale of Neath in 1819, but the most famous of these visiting artists was the great J.M.W. Turner, who painted Aberdulais Falls.

Waterfall Country

The Vale of Neath is often referred to as waterfall country - a reflection of the fact that here there are more waterfalls concentrated into one small area than in any other part of Wales.

The best-known and most accessible falls are those at Melincourt and Aberdulais, as well as the seventeen enchanting cascades created at Gnoll Country Park, Neath, by Herbert Mackworth in 1740. These three attractions are described more fully on pages 61, 59 and 63 respectively.

Many more waterfalls are to be found in the wooded valleys and deep gorges of the rivers Mellte, Hepste and Nedd, between the villages of Pontneddfechan and Ystradfellte, on the southern edge of the Brecon Beacons. The only way to see them is on foot, and the car park of the Angel Inn in Pontneddfechan is the ideal starting point.

The easiest of the walks from here is to the falls at Sgwd Gwladus. It takes about 45 minutes each way along a marked footpath, and the lower sections are negotiable by pushchairs. The walk is also suitable for the less abled.

Some of the other eight falls in the area can be more difficult to get to, however, particularly in wet and slippery conditions. So it is well worth referring to two very useful publications, both of which should be available from the Tourist Information Centre in Pontneddfechan.

One is the full-colour booklet *Waterfall Walks in the Vale of Neath*, and the other is the Brecon Beacons National Park leaflet *Waterfall Walks in the Ystradfellte Area*. Also essential to the serious waterfall explorer in the Vale of Neath is the Ordnance Survey Outdoor Leisure Map Number 11.

The nine falls in the Pontneddfechan area are Sgwd Gwladys and Sgwd Einion Gam on the River Pyrddin; Horseshoe Falls, Lower Ddwli Falls and Upper Ddwli Falls on the Neddfechan River; the Sgwd-yr-Eira Falls on the River Hepste; and the falls of Lower, Middle and Upper Clungwyn on the River Mellte.

Each is spectacular in its own way, and if revisited at different times of the year rewards you with new aspects of its natural beauty as the changing seasons alter the face and colour of the landscape.

The National Eisteddfod

To the Welsh, the National Eisteddfod is just as much a part of the annual calendar as is Christmas. Yet while many visitors from outside Wales will have heard of it, far fewer will realise just how much excitement this great festival generates.

The Royal National Eisteddfod, as it is more properly known, is a major cultural festival of music, poetry and the arts. It is unique, probably the largest travelling festival in Europe, and it annually attracts more than 150,000 visitors and 6,000 competitors from all over Wales and beyond.

The venue for the eisteddfod alternates from year to year between North Wales and South Wales. In 1994 it is the turn of the south and the beautiful Vale of Neath.

As is customary, the 9-day event will be held in the first week of August, during which the best of the eisteddfod's Welsh poets, prose writers, singers and musicians will be honoured.

Indeed, the highlights of the eisteddfod are the three major ceremonies themselves. These date back more than 800 years, to the time of the very

NEATH AND DISTRICT
NATIONAL EISTEDDFOD
OF WALES

Royal National Eisteddfod of Wales

It will be the turn of the Neath valley to welcome the National Eisteddfod in August '94, this wonderful peripatetic festival that captures the cultural variety and richness of Wales.

Three major ceremonies, and over 6,000 competitors from singers and dancers, to poets and potters will take to the stage during Eisteddfod week.

Evening concerts will feature some of Wales' finest performers, including the renowned soprano Margaret Price, and acclaimed folk singer Siân James.

Over 300 trade stands ranging from crafts stalls to antiques will complete this wonderful picture.

Complete the coupon, and send for a free colour brochure.

Name: ______________________

Address: ______________________

____

Post Code: ______________________

Send to: Marketing Officer, Eisteddfod Office, 40 Parc Tŷ Glas, Llanishen, Cardiff CF4 5WU
Tel 0222 763777

first National Eisteddfod in 1176. The ceremonies are full of pageantry and colour, the bards dressed in white robes and the Archdruid resplendent in golden crown, cape and Celtic-style breastplate.

The first of the ceremonies is the Crowning of the Bard, the recipient being the writer of the best free-verse poetry. Two days later sees the presentation of the Prose Medal, awarded for prose written to a given theme. And two days after that, on the penultimate day of the eisteddfod, Welsh poetry is honoured again when the winning writer receives the Bardic Chair in the great Chairing ceremony.

In all there are over 200 competitions, including solo and choral singing, verse recitation, and the playing of musical instruments. The competitive programme reaches a dramatic climax on the final Saturday, when the best of Wales' male voice choirs do battle for first, second and third place.

And the sheer diversity of the eisteddfod's musical offerings ensures that there is something here for everyone - from traditional Welsh choral singing to contemporary rock.

The evening concert programme is typical of the variety on offer. On the first Saturday over 500 children from the Neath area will present an original musical, followed on Sunday evening by world-famous soprano Dame Margaret Price in a performance of Verdi's Requiem.

The nucleus of the eisteddfod, which is built on an open field, is the main pavilion. This can comfortably accommodate up to 4,000 people and provides centre stage for most of the festival's competitions, concerts and ceremonies.

Surrounding the main pavilion is a cluster of smaller pavilions, serving a variety of purposes. For example, here you can see Wales' largest arts and crafts exhibition and a separate exhibition of science and technology. There is also a literature pavilion, a theatre, a youth pavilion pulsating with non-stop music and entertainment, a dance hall, and a pavilion for learners of the Welsh language.

Completing the scene are more than 300 individual trade units and stands selling Welsh crafts, books and music. There are also creche and play areas, picnic areas, comfortable undercover food patios tempting you with everything from crepes to candyfloss, and even banking facilities. Not surprisingly in a major festival of this nature, all the major Welsh institutions - from the Wales Tourist Board to Welsh Water - are exhibiting here too.

It is easy to understand why the Royal National Eisteddfod is the major cultural festival in the Welsh calendar. It is all about preserving Wales' identity and unique character, and though the language of the pavilion events is Welsh a special English translation service is provided free of charge. So no one, regardless of language or nationality, need feel excluded from this spectacular festival of celebration. Facilities for the disabled also ensure that wheelchairs have access to all pavilions.

In 1995 the National Eisteddfod moves north to Colwyn Bay, returns south to Llandeilo in 1996, and for 1997 will be held at Bala, in the south-east corner of the Snowdonia National Park. Each location will mark the event by setting up a circle of undressed local stone, as is the tradition.

Gwydion Roberts

The 1994 National Eisteddfod at a glance

Date:	Saturday 30th July to Saturday 6th August inclusive.
Location:	Near Glynneath, Vale of Neath, on the main A465.
Ceremonies:	Crowning of the Bard (Monday 1st August). Presentation of the Prose Medal (Wednesday 3rd August). Chairing of the Bard (Friday 5th August).
Choir Competitions:	Mixed choirs, 41-60 voices (Saturday 30th July). Mixed choirs, over 61 voices (Monday 1st August). Pensioners' choirs (Tuesday 2nd August). Ladies' choirs (Wednesday 3rd August). Mixed choirs, up to 40 voices (Friday 5th August). Male voice choirs, 3 classes (Saturday 6th August).

ATTRACTIONS & PLACES OF INTEREST

Penscynor Wildlife Park

This is no ordinary wildlife park - if there is such a thing - because Penscynor has earned an international reputation for its conservation work, and particularly for the care and captive breeding of endangered parrots, primates and other species.

Nor is the park concerned only with animals. It has many other attractions which make this a great family day out, and it currently draws in more than 250,000 visitors a year.

Furthermore, Penscynor's evolution from a semi-derelict house into a wildlife sanctuary of such international importance could hardly be described as conventional.

It all began in 1966, when local builder and wildlife film-maker Idris Hale purchased Penscynor House. Before long the 11-acre grounds were home to a large collection of exotic parrots - Idris's life-long passion. So impressive was this bird menagerie that an increasing number of people asked to see it. Idris obliged by holding charity open days, before taking the momentous decision to become a serious visitor attraction and open the doors to the public. This he did in 1971, and TV personality Johnny Morris, of *Animal Magic* fame, officially opened the park, which by this time was also home to several species of mammal.

Success was not slow to arrive, as the park soon collected major tourist awards, acceptance to

Penscynor Wildlife Park

the National Federation of Zoological Gardens, and an ever-increasing number of appreciative visitors.

Within a few years several acres of the adjoining larch plantation had been acquired and developed, and the installation of the now-famous chairlift and alpine slide boosted attendances still further and generated much-needed income for the programme of wildlife conservation upon which Idris had embarked.

Today this programme has grown to such an extent that Penscynor is involved in many international initiatives for species conservation. High on the agenda are primates, such as the golden lion tamarins - small, brilliantly-coloured monkeys - some of which have been born and reared in the park and subsequently released into their native Brazilian forests. The success of the reptile breeding programme has also seen Round Island skinks returned to Mauritius as part of the plan to reintroduce them to their original habitat. Meanwhile, many other species must wait until secure refuges have been established before they can be reintroduced into the wild.

Penscynor also supports several international field projects, and currently the most urgent concern is Proyecto Titi. This project is working hard to understand the ecology of the Colombian rainforest and to persuade people of the value of the forest's wildlife. Under great threat is the cotton-topped tamarin, a squirrel-sized monkey with a critically-endangered wild population, though the park has succeeded in establishing a stable captive population.

Like every good zoo and wildlife park, Penscynor is constantly striving to increase our knowledge and understanding of all species, and to raise awareness of the need for conservation. Consequently, there is a great commitment to education and research. In 1976 the Penscynor Education Department was established, in 1987 the first full-time Education Officer was appointed, and in 1989 the Zoo Centre was opened - a purpose-built lecture theatre, classroom and exhibition centre. The idea of formal teaching for school groups has now evolved into a more active approach to informing and educating all the park's visitors, regardless of age, by means of animal-handling sessions, question and answer sessions, feeding-time talks and so on.

You can also play your part in conservation by adopting an animal at the park. In return for a small fee, you receive a factsheet about your chosen animal, an adoption certificate, a plaque (which is mounted on the animal's cage or enclosure), and an end-of-year report on the animal's progress.

Of course, by no means every visitor to Penscynor Wildlife Park will be a wildlife enthusiast; many come simply to enjoy the other attractions. These include a chairlift over the tree tops, with a return trip down the alpine slide on a wheeled toboggan; radio-controlled cars and boats; bumper cars and a children's playground with bouncy castle; waterfalls and gardens; a souvenir shop; the Copper Kettle Coffee Shop (open all year); the Burger Restaurant (seasonal); picnic areas; and, of course, the animals! Within the park's 16 acres are 100 species of exotic birds, 25 species of monkey, a small aquarium and reptile house, penguins, sea lions, deer, otters,

Wales Tourist Board

flamingos and many more fascinating creatures.

Penscynor Wildlife Park is open every day of the year except Christmas Day. It is located at Cilfrew, 2 miles north of Neath, on the A465. For more information ring 0639 642189.

Gunsmoke Cowboy Town & Seven Sisters Sawmill and Museum

This award-winning double attraction is in the Dulais Valley, 11 miles north of Neath, on the A4109. The miniature cowboy town of Gunsmoke is a sheer delight for children, with a Fort Apache, a saloon and jailhouse, mock shoot-outs between cowboys, a daring free train ride through Gunsmoke County, and guns for all young deputies. You can also visit Honeysuckle Grove and own a Welsh cottage for a day in a street where the houses are three-quarters normal size. And there is plenty to see in the Seven Sisters Sawmill and Museum, such as the development of woodworking methods and machinery, the evolution of mining lamps from the 18th century to the present day, and demonstrations in the working sawmill of how modern techniques of timber cutting compare with the old. Parking is free, and there are picnic areas and refreshments. For more details ring 0639 700288.

Cefn Coed Colliery Museum

The museum stands on the site of the old colliery and portrays the story of the men and machines who mined coal from what was the world's deepest anthracite mine. On show is the massive steam winding engine which once lowered and raised the cages in the shaft, along with the 6 huge boilers that powered it. There is an underground mining gallery, reconstructing life at the coalface; an exhibition area tracing the mining and social history of the valleys; outdoor exhibits which include winding headgear and a colliery loco; a souvenir shop; and, in peak summertime, a tea room. The Cefn Coed Colliery Museum is near Crynant in the Dulais Valley. Ring 0639 750556 for further information.

Aberdulais Falls

Now owned by the National Trust, the impressive Aberdulais Falls are set within a small, picturesque wooded gorge alongside the River Dulais. This is one of the most famous waterfalls in the Vale of Neath, and it is also an important industrial archaeological site. Since 1584 water has been harnessed here to provide power for a variety of industries - copper smelting, ironworks, a cornmill and tinplate works among them.

The unique new hydro-electric Turbine House - the result of a long-term conservation programme by the National Trust - now gives visitors access to the top of the falls, including wheelchair access for the disabled. Nearby, in the wheel pit of the restored Victorian tinplate works, is Britain's largest electricity-generating waterwheel, over 26 feet in diameter. This enormous wheel is a replica of the 1830's original, which drove the rolling mills for reducing wrought iron bars into thin sheets for tinning.

For hundreds of years the splendour and drama of Aberdulais Falls has attracted artists and writers, and many works by landscape painters such as Turner are on display in the Visitor Information Centre. On site there is also a National Trust gift shop. For more information ring 0639 636674.

Melincourt Falls

Located just outside Resolven, Melincourt

Wales Tourist Board

Waterfalls Reserve is owned and managed by Glamorgan Wildlife Trust. The spectacular falls, on a tributary of the River Neath, are 80 feet high and were captured on canvas by Turner in 1794. The reserve itself includes 12 acres of broad-leaved woodland comprising mature durmast oak, gnarled silver birch, wild cherry, rowan and crab apple, and alder. In spring the woodland floor is a carpet of bluebells. This humid narrow valley is also home to an interesting variety of birds. Redstart, wood warbler and pied flycatcher are common in summer, and dipper and grey wagtail can be seen along the stream throughout the year. In the northern part of the reserve are the remains of a 17th-century blast furnace and ironworks. These works, in production for 100 years, had a great overshot waterwheel which was powered by water carried in a channel from above the falls. A car park at the entrance to the village of Clyne, on the B4434 one mile south of Resolven, marks the start of a 15-minute walk to see the falls.

Neath Canal, Resolven

Together the Neath and Tennant Canals form a 21-mile waterway between Glynneath and Swansea. A 4-mile stretch of the Neath Canal above Resolven has been restored, and the landscaped towpath provides a very pleasant countryside walk which takes in 7 locks, 2 aqueducts, 4 bridges, and canal basins at both Resolven and Aberdulais. At the latter, which marks the meeting point of the two canal systems, you will also find a restored skew bridge and a 10-arched aqueduct - a feature which makes this site unique in Wales.

Two barges, the *Thomas Dadford* and the *Enfys*, offer trips from Resolven during summer months, and the *Enfys* has been fitted out to take less-abled passengers. Another attraction is a restored 18th-century lengthsman's cottage, *Ty Banc*, which is now a tearoom and gift shop.

And it is not only people who are enjoying the canal's new lease of life. This is also an important wildlife reserve, providing wetlands for marsh and aquatic plants and a variety of birds, including kingfisher and heron.

For more information about the Neath Canal

Neath Abbey

Mike Collier

and its attractions, ring 0639 641121 or visit the Tourist Information Centres in Aberdulais or Pontneddfechan.

Old gunpowder factory and the Dinas Silica Mines, Pontneddfechan

The area around the village of Pontneddfechan, famous for its waterfalls, was at one time also a thriving centre of industry and innovation. The Gunpowder Works, established in 1857 by the Vale of Neath Powder Company, was located on the banks of the River Mellte and stretched for a mile and a half up the valley. The site was ideal - firstly because of its remoteness in relation to the potential danger of gunpowder manufacture, and secondly because of its proximity to an abundance of trees for charcoal and the power of the river to drive the factory's machinery. The gunpowder produced on the 180-acre site was used mainly in coal mines and quarries. The remains of many of the works' buildings can still be seen.

Silica rock, or quartzite, was mined commercially in the Pontneddfechan area during a 150-year period from the late 18th century until 1964. The silica mines stood near Dinas Rock, where the quartzite was first discovered in the 1780's. Just 2 miles away was the Pontwalby Brickworks, where William Weston Young exploited the potential of silica - an extremely hard rock which has few impurities and a high melting point - by using it to manufacture the famous Dinas fire-brick. Silica mined at Pontneddfechan was also supplied to the Landore Brickworks in Swansea. The remains of the mines' old levels and tramroads can still be seen on the banks of the rivers Mellte and Neddfechan.

Neath Abbey

This Cistercian abbey, originally affiliated to the monastic order of Savigny, was founded in 1130 on a rocky terrace overlooking the river marshlands. It became one of the richest of all Welsh monasteries, and was described as "the fairest abbey in all Wales" by the Tudor historian John Leland. With typical Cistercian enterprise, it acquired very extensive land and property holdings, large numbers of sheep, horses and cattle, and commercial interests which included shipping, mills, fisheries and coal mines. But by the 1530's only eight monks remained here, and after the Dissolution of the Monasteries by Henry VIII in 1536 the abbey was vandalised and fell into disuse and decay. New life was breathed into it in the 18th century when it was converted into a large mansion. Part of the abbey was even used as a furnace for a copperworks, as proven by scorch marks which are still visible on a wall.

The abbey stands on the banks of the Tennant Canal amidst an industrialised and urbanised landscape. Yet it still maintains an air of tranquility which visitors find hard to resist. It is open all year round and is now in the care of Cadw (Welsh Historic Monuments), though Neath Antiquarian Society has carried out restoration work on both the abbey and Neath Castle.

Neath Borough Museum

Neath Musem stands in the heart of the town, only 5 minutes' walk from the bus and train stations. The beautifully-refurbished building it occupies is Grade II listed, designed in 1847 by Alfred Russell Wallace as a Mechanics' Institute to provide elementary and technical education. The museum has been created to promote the borough's fascinating historical, industrial, archaeological and cultural heritage. In the upper gallery are displays depicting the natural history and archaeology of the district, and a medieval exhibition illustrates the histories of Neath Castle and Neath Abbey. The lower gallery is reserved for temporary exhibitions. The museum also has a shop selling books, postcards and souvenirs. Admission to the museum, which opens all year round, is free. Ring 0639 645741 for further information.

Craig Gwladus Country Park

Lying between Penscynor Wildlife Park and Neath golf course, the country park is just one mile long and only a fifth of a mile wide at its broadest point. Yet it rises to 500 feet above sea level and gives spectacular views over the Dulais and lower Neath valleys. The park has an extensive area of woodland, which ranges from oak and Japanese larch to beech and conifer, and there are waymarked footpaths and picnic areas to enjoy. The park provides a habitat for a great variety of birds, including woodpecker, tree-creeper, nuthatch, sparrowhawk, buzzard and barn owl.

Gnoll Country Park

The gardens of Gnoll Park, now recognised as the most important 18th-century landscaped gardens in Wales, are owned and managed by Neath Borough Council and are open free of charge during daylight hours. The park was originally owned and created by the Mackworth family, wealthy industrialists who first came to Neath in 1686. There are many interesting and enchanting features here - ponds, cascades, bridges, towers, and even a folly, the Ivy Tower, built in 1795. The most impressive spectacle is provided by the seventeen cascades, which rush down the hill into the Mosshouse reservoir. The former icehouse and the remains of the Gnoll House have been restored, and recreational facilities include a children's playground and a 9-hole pitch and putt golf course.

Eaglesbush Valley

A tranquil woodland area, following a river valley, which provides a green and pleasant walk within

Below: Coal & Steam Centre, Neath Valley

Wales Tourist Board

the densely populated area of Melincrythan.

Pant-y-Sais Fen

This is an SSSI (Site of Special Scientific Interest) and also a designated Nature Reserve. It is situated in the centre of the village of Jersey Marine, just south-west of Neath and close to the shoreline of Swansea Bay, and a car park and boardwalks give access to the fenland. There are many species of wildlife here.

Dan-Yr-Ogof Showcaves

A major tourist attraction, the showcave complex is the largest in Western Europe and is located midway between Swansea and Brecon on the A4067, within the Brecon Beacons National Park. The winner of no less than 10 important tourism awards, the showcaves feature the longest showcave in Britain; the Cathedral Showcave - largest single chamber in any British showcave; Bone Cave - home of Bronze Age man 3000 years ago; the Dinosaur Park; a museum and audio visual theatre; a craft shop and information centre; a coffee shop and covered picnic area; and an artificial ski slope and instruction. Nearby is the Craig-y-Nos Country Park, and 12 miles away is the National Park's Mountain Centre. For more information on the showcaves ring 0639 730284 or 730693.

Concerts

Gwyn Hall, Neath, hosts a varied and interesting programme of concerts throughout year. Ring 0639 641121 for up-to-date information.

Neath Fair

The oldest and biggest fair of its kind in Wales, Neath Fair is an exciting and colourful 4-day event held every year in the second week of September.

SPORTS & ACTIVITIES

There are many opportunities for visitors to the Vale of Neath to enjoy sports, leisure and recreational activities. The following is a guide to some of the facilities available.

Boating

Boats up to 500mm draft can be accommodated on the Neath Canal. Ring 0639 641121.

Bowls

There are 5 bowling greens at various locations throughout the borough.

Cricket

Neath Cricket Club plays at The Gnoll ground in the centre of the town, a venue it shares with the All Blacks rugby club. Glamorgan County Cricket Club also make regular appearances at The Gnoll, taking on touring national teams such as Australia and the West Indies. For match and other details ring Neath Cricket Club on 0639 643719.

Fishing

Game fishing is available in the Neath and Dulais rivers, and coarse fishing in the Neath and Tennant canals and the Gnoll grounds. For other venues contact:

Glynneath & District Angling Association (0639 720219).

Neath and Dulais Angling Club (0639 710655).

Tackle & Bait, 42 Windsor Road, Neath (0639 634148).

Golf

Golfers are particularly well catered for in the Vale of Neath, with a choice of 6 courses.

Swansea Bay Golf Course: An 18-hole course at Jersey Marine overlooking Swansea Bay. Tel:0792 812198.

Earlswood Golf Course: A new 18-hole course above the existing Swnasea Bay course. Rounds are on a pay-and-play basis. 0792 321578.

Neath Golf Course: An 18-hole course and one of the highest in Wales, giving views which take in 7 counties! 0639 643615

Glynneath Golf Club: An 18-hole course at Pontneddfechan, in the foothills of the Brecon Beacons. 0639 720452.

Glyn Clydach House Hotel, Neath : A 9-hole pitch and putt course. 0792 818411.

Gnoll Park: A 9-hole pitch and putt course. Enquiries: 0639 641121

Pelenna Mountain Centre

Spectacularly located in the hills above Tonmawr, this outdoor pursuits centre offers an exciting choice of residential courses throughout the year. For more information ring 0639 636227.

Pony trekking

Pant y Sais Riding Centre, Jersey Marine: Pony trekking along the Jersey Marine shoreline. Tel: 0792 813213.

Moss House Reservoir: Ring Byron Jones, Wenallt Farm, Tonna on 0639 630836.

Cimla Pony Trekking Centre: Ring Hawdref Ganol Farm on 0639 631884.

Rugby

Neath's rugby team, known as the All Blacks, is one of the top five club sides in Wales and regularly has players chosen to represent Wales at international level. The club's ground is The Gnoll in the centre of Neath. For fixture details ring 0639 639684.

Sailing

Monkstone Marina, on the River Neath at Briton Ferry, has a clubhouse and also offers berths for hire. Ring 0792 812229.

Swimming and sports centres

Neath Leisure Centre: Located in Dyfed Road in the centre of Neath, this recently-refurbished leisure centre has a swimming pool, hydroslide, sauna, solarium, squash courts and many more facilities.

Glynneath: Swimming pool, multigym and canoe training. Ring 0639 720345 for opening times.

Llangatwg School: Swimming pool with limited opening hours. Ring 0639 720345.

Neath Sports Centre: Major facilities such as an athletics track, all-weather sports pitches and a sports hall.

Hengwrt Sports Hall, Briton Ferry: Most indoor sporting pursuits catered for.

Tennis

There are 6 courts at Neath Leisure Centre and 3 courts at Jersey Park, Briton Ferry.

Walking

The Vale of Neath gives walkers plenty of opportunities, including Pant y Sais Fen, Melin Cwrt Falls, Neath and Tennant canals, Coed Morgannwg Way, Sarn Helen, Eaglesbush Valley, Longford Dingle, Shelone Woods, waterfall walks and Forestry Commission walks.

Below:
Dan-Yr-Ogof Showcaves

Wales Tourist Board

Port Talbot & The Afan Valley

Anyone driving west along the M4 towards Gower and seeing the unsightly spread of Port Talbot's steel and chemical works could be forgiven for thinking that this is not the ideal place to spend a holiday.

Yet this apparently uninviting panorama is one of South Wales' biggest deceptions. Because just minutes away you will find not only two of the finest stretches of beach along the coastline, namely Aberavon and Margam Sands, but also the astonishingly beautiful Afan Valley - possibly the most picturesque valley in the whole of Wales. And leaving the M4 at junctions 38 or 40 to discover them for yourself could prove to be one of the best decisions of your holiday.

As well as the superb beaches, there are other major attractions in this unlikely holiday region.

One is Margam Park, where Margam Castle was once home to the Talbot family who gave their name to Port Talbot. Another is the Afan Argoed Country Park, which is an excellent starting point for exploring the glorious Afan Valley by any number of means - on foot, horseback, bike or Landrover. Within the country park is the fascinating Welsh Miners' Museum - originally the vision and single-handed creation of a remarkable ex-miner.

The Borough of Port Talbot

As with Llanelli, the name Port Talbot refers not only to a town but also to a borough; in this case an area of 40,000 acres, extending from Swansea Bay to the head of the Afan Valley beyond Glyncorrwg.

It is a region of great contrasts. Away from the narrow coastal plain - into which is concentrated the borough's industry, motorway and the majority of its population - mountains rise to a height of 1700 feet above wooded countryside, offering sweeping views of Swansea Bay and the Bristol Channel. The mountains also form an effective barrier against prevailing winds and are a contributory factor to Port Talbot's mild climate.

The history of the area can be traced back at least 4000 years. There is evidence of occupation here in the Neolithic Age, and traces of Bronze Age and Iron Age tumuli and hillforts can be seen at Mynydd y Gaer (Baglan), Pen-y-Castell (Ynysygwas), and Bwlwarcau (North Margam). The discovery of four inscribed stones is also proof that a Roman road ran through what is now Port Talbot, and other important historical finds include two 6th-century stones with Ogham characters which are now in the Stones Museum at Margam Abbey. The great Wheel Cross of Conbelin is also in the museum, along with other Celtic stones and crosses.

In more recent history, Port Talbot - or Port Aberavon as it was known until the 19th century - has been a seaport for many centuries. Today, the town of Port Talbot is the "capital" and administrative centre of the borough.

The town centre, much of which was late Victorian and early Edwardian, has been redeveloped on both sides of the River Afan. On the west bank is the new Civic Centre, which houses the Princess Royal Theatre - an important

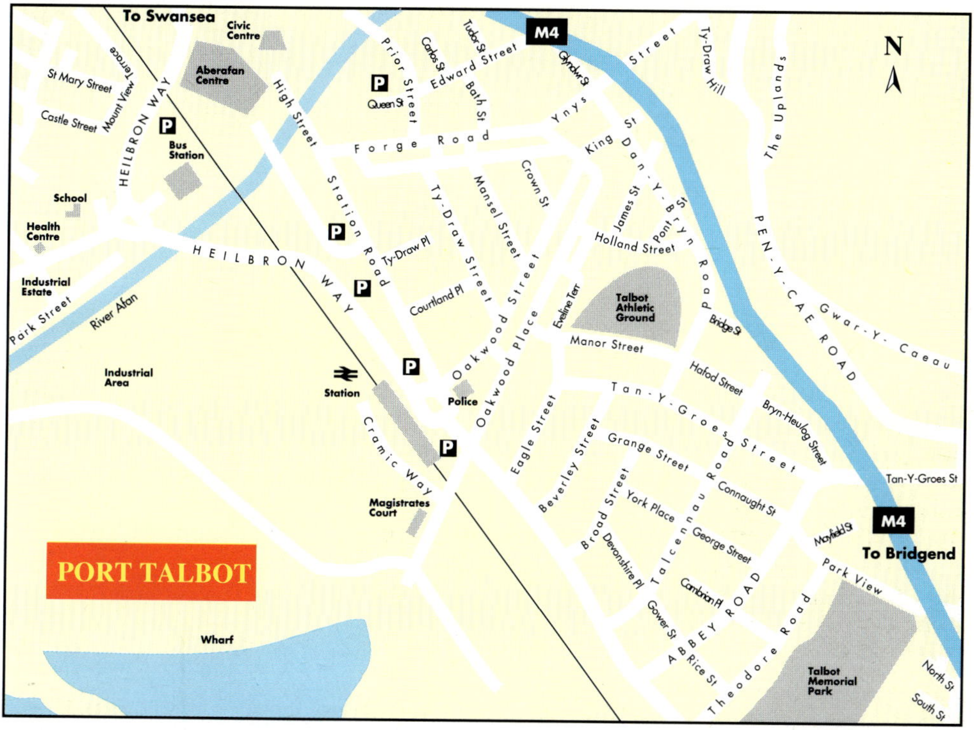

venue for a wide variety of international entertainment, as well as for fashion shows and other major events. Nearby, the Aberafan Shopping Centre is a climatically-controlled complex with a good choice of shops and an indoor market. There is also an ever-popular outdoor market, held on Tuesdays and Saturdays at the rear of Station Road. On the opposite side of the river, the east bank, is the town's attractive pedestrianised shopping thoroughfare.

Despite its industry, the borough of Port Talbot is still largely rural and the economy is dominated by the town and its suburbs of Baglan, Aberavon, Taibach and Margam.

Baglan

Baglan lies to the north-west of the town and until modern times was a rural retreat of great beauty. It was a place much loved by poets and novelists, notably Charles Kingsley and R.D. Blackmore, and though urbanised through residential development some parts of Baglan still enjoy panoramic views of Swansea Bay. There are also pleasant parklands to be found here, including the grounds which originally belonged to Baglan Hall. In these grounds is a fine collection of trees representing every continent of the world. Also boasting interesting features is St. Catherine's Church.

Taibach

Situated south-east of the town, Taibach developed round the original steelworks of Port Talbot. Major investment in the plant, the most recent of which was completed in 1986 and officially opened by the Prince and Princess of Wales, has established it as one of the most modern steelworks in Europe.

In sharp contrast, Taibach has strong connections with the arts. The brilliant Sir Anthony Hopkins was born here, and this is also the home of the Afan Arts Centre - an Elizabethan-style round theatre much favoured for art and photographic exhibitions.

Margam

Margam is residential on its western side, where the steelworks of Port Talbot separate it from the shoreline, and rural on its eastern side, where it

Pontrhydyfen Viaduct

Wales Tourist Board

encompasses Margam Country Park and extends to Ogwr on the borough boundaries. Margam Country Park is widely regarded as one of the best in Wales. It is based around the castle and the abbey, and offers a great variety of attractions. Nearby is Eglwys Nunydd Reservoir, a popular centre for sailing and fishing, and behind Margam is the ideal riding and pony trekking country of the Goytre Valley.

Cwmafan

Though now a prosperous residential area of Port Talbot, this was once a major industrial centre - the site of coke ovens, tinplate works and the English Copper Company.

Port Talbot's industrial revolution

The opening of a copper-smelting works in 1770 marked the beginning of two centuries of industrial growth for what was then Port Aberavon. The port facilities were well placed to receive shipments of copper ore from the nearby Cornish coast, and the area around the harbour grew at such a pace that it soon became a town in its own right.

In 1836 the town was renamed Port Talbot. This was in honour of the Talbot family of Margam Castle - pioneers of the booming industry, and owners of most of the land on which the town and docks were built.

Further prosperity for Port Talbot arrived with the railways. Coal exports grew and the port became a major distribution point for many of the coalmining villages of the Rhondda Valley. The Port Talbot Railway itself opened in 1897, followed in 1898 by a new modern dock to serve the coalfields and to import iron and copper.

It was not until 1946 that a steelworks was established in Port Talbot - an enterprise which brought welcome relief from the effects of mine closures in the Afan and surrounding valleys. By 1970 this had become the largest steelworks in Britain; today it is one of the most modern in Europe, though the number of people it employs has dropped drastically in recent years.

Port Talbot's importance as an industrial centre and major port was further underlined in the 1970's with the commissioning of Britain's biggest deep-water harbour. This now provides the deepest berthing facility in the Bristol Channel

Margam Castle

Margam Park

and can comfortably accommodate vessels well in excess of 100,000 tons.

Aberavon

Aberavon stands between Port Talbot and the sea on the eastern shore of Swansea Bay. Its origins go way back to the 12th century. At that time a Norman castle, of which nothing now remains, guarded a strategic crossing point of the River Afan, and in 1304 the granting of a royal charter established Aberavon as a medieval borough in its own right. Today, of course, it is part of the modern borough of Port Talbot.

In the fifties and sixties, Aberavon was a very popular venue for day trippers who came from the town and the valleys to enjoy its superb sandy beach. This is more than two miles long, very wide, and regarded as one of the finest surfing beaches in South Wales. At one end it stretches to the Neath estuary, at the other to Port Talbot docks; beyond the docks is yet more beautiful and apparently unending beach in the shape of Margam Sands.

The promenade and the Afan Lido leisure centre add to Aberavon's attraction, though limited infrastructure and lack of accommodation means that it has never competed as a full-blown seaside resort. But now major redevelopment of the whole Aberavon seafront is to be undertaken, and work has already begun on transforming the Afan Lido into a state-of-the-art leisure complex which will satisfy the demands of the twenty-first century.

This ambitious scheme is an exercise not only in engineering skill and ingenuity but also in landscaping on a grand scale, as it requires the construction of two huge artificial headlands on the Aberavon shoreline. They will stand about one mile apart and extend a considerable distance seaward, thereby creating a bay in which a large section of the beach will sit.

The idea is to rejuvenate the beach and return it to its former level, because since the sea wall of the promenade was built the effects of wave action have removed large quantities of sand from one end of the beach and deposited excessive amounts at the other end. The beach has also suffered from

Blaengwynfi

Wales Tourist Board

Brace Harvatt Associates

coal deposits - originating from undersea seams - and this problem too will be eliminated.

Devising the solution to these problems was an engineering feat in itself. It necessitated the building of an exact replica of Aberavon beach and seafront, in the form of a scale model and a sophisiticated wave tank, so that the pattern and effects of wave action along the shoreline could be accurately duplicated.

The two new headlands, which will be complemented by two smaller groynes along the seafront, will also provide additional benefits as areas for walking and fishing and as excellent vantage points for spectacular views over Swansea Bay.

The redevelopment plans include the creation of a new 9-hole golf course on the waterfront and an area designated for bathing, boating and sailboarding. Landscaping and formal gardens will be other major features, as will commercial and residential development. There is even provision for two new hotels.

However, next to the new-look beach the main attraction to visitors will be the superb new Afan Lido. When the original was built in the 1960's it was the last word in leisure centres - but it's obvious from the plans that you ain't seen nothing yet!

The new Afan Lido will be nothing less than an all-weather water theme park - one of the major sports and leisure facilities in Wales. The leisure pool, for example, will boast a wave machine, geysers, water jets, fountains and slides. There will also be a 25-metre, 8-lane gala pool; a unisex changing village with facilities for families and disabled sports enthusiasts; a health and fitness suite with sauna, steam, solarium and treatment rooms; and full facilities for spectators.

Work on this massive scheme to rejuvenate the Aberavon seafront is due to start in 1995 and will continue beyond the year 2000.

But you don't have to wait that long before you visit Aberavon. The sandy beach offers safe bathing and is excellent for windsurfing, surfing, canoeing and other watersports.

Backing the beach is the promenade, with its

sunken gardens, boating and paddling pools, play equipment, and easy parking just 50 yards from the sands.

And though Afan Lido is already under reconstruction, some of the facilities remain open. For up-to-date information you can ring Port Talbot's public relations office on 0639 875313, or Afan Lido direct on 0639 884141.

The Afan Valley

Aberavon and its superb beach is not the only surprise awaiting you in the borough of Port Talbot. There is also the winding, picturesque, singularly beautiful Afan Valley - the narrowest of all the Welsh mining valleys.

Through it runs the River Afan, only twelve miles long, rising west of the Rhondda Valley and snaking its way down to Aberavon to merge with the waters of Swansea Bay and the Bristol Channel.

From the early 19th century until just twenty-five years ago, the Afan Valley was famous for its coal and for the railways which carried it to the docks at Port Talbot. The last mine closed in 1971. Since then the hillsides laid barren by mining operations have been replanted, and large areas of new coniferous woodland have earned the valley the name of Little Switzerland. The similarities are clear to see: forested hills, the steep-sided valley, fast-flowing streams and panoramic views. Such scenic beauty is a miracle of land reclamation, and the network of forestry tracks makes it easy to experience and appreciate it first hand.

Yet not all evidence of the valley's long dependence on coal has disappeared. The villages still retain much of their unique character, and at Cymmer there is a permanent reminder of the valley's once-extensive railway network, the refreshment room of the old station having been converted into a pub of the same name.

Then there is the Welsh Miners Museum in the Afan Argoed Country Park. The museum gives a vivid portrayal of what life was like for the men and children who toiled deep underground in the valley's pits, and of the hardships endured by the

Margam Park

Afan Argoed

small mining communities.

One son of the valley who exchanged a working life at the coal face for a glittering career on stage and film was the late great Richard Burton. He was born in the village of Pontrhydyfen, where the valley is so constricted that viaducts and aqueducts provided the only routes by which coal could be transported.

Tha Afan Valley today is a sheer delight for anyone who has a yen to explore miles of forested countryside. The only problem is that like Richard Burton himself, it is a very tough act to follow.

ATTRACTIONS & PLACES OF INTEREST

Afan Argoed Country Park

The park is set in acres of unspoiled woodland and is the gateway to exploring the Afan Valley. If you choose to go on foot there are plenty of waymarked footpaths, including the 27-mile Coed Morgannwg Way, which links the park with Margam Park and Rhigos mountain. For the really keen there is also a wayfaring/orienteering course, while the less ambitious will be content with the picturesque riverside walk. Or you can hire a mountain bike and escape along any of the 14 miles of bike routes, which are mainly off road and take you through beautiful countryside. Another alternative is to hop aboard the Landrover and enjoy spectacular views as you trek through the forests.

Focal point of the park is the Countryside Centre. Here you will find information, guide books to the park, a forests walk leaflet, gifts and souvenirs, and exhibitions on the history of Afan Valley and its wildlife and forestry. The building also houses the Welsh Miners Museum (see next entry).

Other facilities in the park include refreshments, picnic sites, a barbecue area, an adventure playground, camping, and a small touring caravan site. Disabled visitors are well catered for too. For example, there is free loan of electric wheelchairs and the miners museum has braille information panels.

The Afan Argoed Country Park is 6 miles north-east of Port Talbot on the A4107 (exit 40 M4) and is open all year. For more information ring 0639 850564.

Welsh Miners Museum

Located in the Afan Argoed Country Park, the museum was created by local miners in 1976 and vividly portrays the days when coal mining was a way of life in the South Wales valleys. The enlightening displays include contemporary photographs, mining equipment, a scene from a typical miner's cottage, and a mining gallery. Outdoor exhibits feature a pit-head wheel, a haulage engine and a coal tram. For more information about the museum and its opening times ring the Afan Argoed Country Park on 0639 850564.

Margam Country Park

Only 2 miles east of Port Talbot on the A48 (exit 38 M4), historic Margam Country Park is one of the major attractions of South Wales and promises a very full day out.

It comprises 850 acres of open parkland and forest, and has a great variety of things to see and do, from ancient monuments to walks and wildlife.

For example, historic sights here include a 7-acre Iron Age hillfort and the ruins of 12th-century Margam Abbey, which was founded in 1147 and built by Cistercian monks. The abbey was once a great centre of learning, and the copy of the Domesday Book now held by the British Museum was one of the abbey's manuscripts.

In summer there is limited access to Margam Abbey church and Stones Museum, where you can see an important collection of Celtic stones and crosses.

Margam Castle, a Tudor/Gothic-style mansion house completed in 1840, was the home of the Talbot family of Port Talbot fame. It was gutted by fire in 1977 and is now being restored. Another building of great interest is the magnificent 18th-century Orangery, one of the largest in Britain, constructed originally to house orange trees. It is now restored to its former glory and is a venue for major functions.

The park is notable for its collection of work by internationally-renowned sculptors, which is displayed at various points throughout the park. Another intriguing feature is the maze - one of the largest in the world, covering an acre and comprising more than 3000 cypress trees which took four years to reach the required height.

There is also a fascinating variety of wildlife to be found around the park, such as the 600-strong deer herd - the biggest in South Wales - and a herd of Glamorgan cattle. This is now a rare breed and attempts are being made to re-establish it. Local wildlife is well represented in the shape of foxes, badgers, grey squirrels, buzzards, kestrels and sparrowhawks, and along the farm trail you will meet geese, ducks, goats, donkeys, Shetland ponies, rabbits, and several varieties of sheep and pigs. Then there's Fairytaleland - a scaled-down nursery rhyme village for under 8's.

Activities in the park include pony rides and pony trekking, waymarked walks, putting, giant chess and draughts, a road train, and a garden trail for the disabled. The Coach House Theatre shows an interesting 20-minute programme about the park and its history, and has indoor exhibitions and a souvenir and bookshop. Charlotte's Pantry, the Tea Pavilion and Cornet Castle offer a tasty choice of refreshments.

In addition, the park puts on a programme of special events throughout the year. For further information (the park is open all year) ring 0639 881635.

Tollgate Park, Port Talbot

The park now contains the Beulah Chapel - an unusual building noted for its architectural style - which was built in the village of Groes but dismantled because it stood in the path of the M4! It was subsequently transported to Port Talbot and rebuilt in Tollgate Park. Its unique features are the octagonal shape and mullioned windows.

St, Catherine's Church, Baglan

Though building was completed in 1882, the architectural style is 14th century. The church is sometimes referred to as the Alabaster Church because a lavish amount of Penarth alabaster was used in its construction. Notable features include a medieval font, a fine alabaster reredos, and stained glass by Burne-Jones in the east window.

The Orangery, Margam Park

Margam Park

Princess Royal Theatre

Located in Port Talbot's town centre, this 800-seat theatre hosts a variety of top acts, plays and shows and regularly provides a stage for many of the world's stars. The theatre also doubles as a venue for fashion shows, exhibitions and other major events. For details of forthcoming attractions ring 0639 875214.

Afan Lido Concert Hall

Housed in the Lido's huge sports hall, this venue seats 2,500 and offers excellent facilities. As with the Princess Royal Theatre, the concert hall provides the very best in top-name entertainment throughout the year. For details of forthcoming attractions ring 0639 875214 or 0639 884141.

SPORTS & ACTIVITIES

Sports enthusiasts and lovers of the great outdoors will find plenty to do within the borough of Port Talbot. The following is a guide to the facilities and activities available.

Afan Lido Leisure Complex

As described on page 71, the Afan Lido is to be transformed in line with the Aberavon seafront redevelopment scheme, and as work progresses certain facilities will obviously become unavailable. For example, at the time of writing the swimming pool is closed under Phase One of the project. For the latest information you should ring 0639 884141 or 0639 875313. However, it is expected that the sports hall will be unaffected for some time, and the facilities here include indoor courts for 5-a-side soccer, netball, hockey, tennis, volley ball, squash and badminton; rooms for table tennis, circuit training, martial arts, judo and gymnastics; a fitness and weight training suite; a 6-rink indoor bowling stadium; and a cafe and bar.

Bowls

There are many bowls teams in Port Talbot and the Afan Valley, so enthusiasts are well catered for here. There are 8 rinks in parks throughout the borough, each maintained to a very high standard.

Cycling

Really fit cyclists can take to the hills, but those in search of more leisurely cycling will be glad to discover that special paths are being created in the Afan Valley on the line of the old railways, with gradients which are not too taxing. It is planned that these paths will eventually form part of a long-distance cycle route, running from Newport to Swansea, aimed at keeping cyclists away from the hazards of busy main roads. Bikes are available for hire from Afan Argoed Country Park.

Fishing

This area is a fisherman's delight. Excellent sea fishing, from Aberavon beach or chartered boats in Swansea Bay, offers tempting catches of cod, ray, conger, bass, monkfish (rock salmon), tope and even shark. Trout fishing is available in Margam Park from April to December, including boat hire, and fly fishing for brown trout and rainbow trout can be enjoyed at Eglwys Nunydd Reservoir.

Golf & putting

There are several golf clubs and courses within easy reach of the area, including Swansea Bay Golf Club, Pyle & Kenfig Golf Club, Royal Porthcawl Golf Club and Maesteg Golf Club. Putting is available in several memorial parks within the borough, namely Bryn, Vivian and Taibach, and also in the Seafront Gardens, Aberavon. Tollgate Park, Margam, has a pitch & putt course.

Riding

The tracks of the area's old railways and the new forestry paths make for first-class riding country, particularly in the peaceful Goytre Valley - home of the L & A Riding Centre. This offers horses and ponies for hire, riding instruction, and even riding holidays, with accommodation in comfortable log cabins. Margam Park is another pony trekking centre. As well as ponies for hire, the park provides donkey rides for the very young during summer months.

Swimming & watersports

In addition to safe bathing off Aberavon beach, swimmers will be able to enjoy the magnificent new pool at Afan Lido (currently being built: see under Afan Lido above). Popular venues for sailing are Swansea Bay (from moorings at the mouth of the River Afan) and the Eglwys Nunydd Reservoir. Boat owners can use the slipway facilities of Port Talbot's Small Boat Club, which also offers moorings for hire.

Brace Harvatt Associates

Tennis

There are 9 tennis courts available within the borough's parks and playing fields.

Walking

The borough of Port Talbot boasts a network of forest tracks and paths and is an excellent area for walking. Margam Park and the Afan Argoed Country Park give access to many outstanding walks, the best-known route being the 27 miles between Margam and Craig y Llyn, which lies above the headwaters of the Rhondda Fawr. For the more ambitious and adventurous, Afan Argoed Country Park also has wayfaring routes which have been laid out in conjunction with the British Orienteering Federation.

Wildlife & the countryside

In an area of vividly contrasting landscapes - wooded valleys, open moorland, forestry plantations, sand dunes and open parkland - there are many places where you can enjoy the countryside and its fascinating wildlife. Remnants of the Afan Valley's original oak and birch woodlands can still be seen, with a rich variety of birds, plants and animals, and newer plantations are attracting their own characteristic birds.

In winter, Eglwys Nunydd Reservoir and the Kenfig Nature Reserve are important feeding grounds for wildfowl.

More about the area's wildlife can be learned from the Countryside Centre in the Afan Argoed Country Park and the Field Studies Centre in Margam Park.

There are also many established picnic sites throughout the area, including Margam Park and Afan Argoed Country Park.

FESTIVALS & EVENTS

Port Talbot Community Festival

This annual summer festival is spread over ten days and provides a bonanza of entertainment. It begins with Fiesta Day and the Grand Parade in the town centre, continuing with fun and festivities in churches, community centres and parks right across the borough. The festival of music and dance at the Princess Royal Theatre guarantees a packed house.

Bonfire & Fireworks Display

A spectacular annual event which is held on Aberavon seafront.

Brace Harvatt Associates

Porthcawl & Ogwr

Porthcawl has been established as a popular seaside resort since the days when the mining communities around Bridgend and the Rhondda valleys first started coming here for their holidays. Today's visitors come in greater numbers and from much further afield. Yet immediately beyond Porthcawl's beaches and attractions is an area of outstanding beauty and interest which is still virtually unknown to all but the people who live within it.

This is the Mid Glamorgan district of Ogwr. A district of compact dimensions, into which is packed an enormous variety of landscape, from towering cliffs and sprawling sand dunes to deep valleys and forested mountains.

Equally diverse is the number and scope of activities which Ogwr lays open to visitors. You can enjoy the beaches of Porthcawl and Southerndown, ride the fun fair of the Coney Beach complex, take in the spectacular cliff scenery of the Heritage Coast, participate in golf or fishing or watersports, get away from it all in the seclusion of Bryngarw Country Park, or take a 15-mile drive north from the coast and suddenly find yourself on dramatic mountain roads a world apart from the lively holiday atmosphere of Porthcawl.

South Porthcawl

Wales Tourist Board

The all-weather recreational facilities in Ogwr are outstanding too, including the largest leisure centre in South Wales and seven indoor swimming pools. Of the district's five top-class golf courses, the Royal Porthcawl is the most famous - one of the best-known links courses in Britain.

And should all of this fail to whet your appetite for Ogwr, there are historic sites and castles, craft workshops, nature reserves, interesting towns and villages, the pretty thatched cottages of Merthyr Mawr, and in Bridgend - Ogwr's largest town - an excellent shopping centre.

Porthcawl

The resort of Porthcawl grew around the little harbour towards the end of the 19th century, tending to the holiday needs of miners from nearby valleys.

The harbour itself existed only because of the coal industry. At its peak in 1873 over 160,000 tons were being shipped out from here each year. But trade declined with the opening of new docks at Barry and Port Talbot, and by 1907 had ceased altogether.

Nearly a century on, the picturesque harbour is busy again. Now the activity is conducted by fishermen and pleasure boats, and sandy Porthcawl has become the most popular spot in Ogwr.

It is very much a family resort, with plenty to offer - a good choice of accommodation, the safe golden beaches of Sandy Bay and Trecco Bay, the huge Coney Beach Amusement Complex, and Europe's biggest caravan park, which has such an extensive range of activities and attractions that it is virtually a resort in its own right.

And with a shoreline ideally suited to watersports, and night-time entertainment provided by clubs, discos and the Grand Pavilion theatre, Porthcawl is nothing if not lively.

Rest Bay

Wales Tourist Board

But Porthcawl is not all donkey rides and ice cream. To the west of the esplanade you can discover the peace and quiet of grassy Lock's Common and the secluded sands and rock pools of appropriately-named Rest Bay. The beaches of this popular surfing venue, which won a Rural Beach Seaside Award in 1993, extend beyond the links of the 18-hole Royal Porthcawl Golf Club to Sker Point. Here you will find Sker House - a local landmark elevated to fame by R.D. Blackmore's novel *The Maid of Sker,* published in 1872.

You will often see Porthcawl described as sandy - and for a very good reason. Apart from its three superb beaches, the resort is surrounded by the vast sand dunes of Kenfig Burrows to the west and Merthyr Mawr Warren to the east.

Fringing the warren is the village of Newton. This has an ancient church and a strange well which is fed by a tidal spring; though inland, the water in the well rises and falls with the changing tides.

Ogmore-by-Sea

Beyond Merthyr Mawr is the village of Ogmore-by-Sea - another popular holiday spot, standing on the rocky shoreline of the Ogmore estuary. The views from here across the widening Bristol Channel are superb, and a little way offshore stands the treacherous Tusker Rock, visible only at low tide and given a wide berth by yachtsmen.

Ogmore-by-Sea marks another dramatic feature in the landscape. From here, the coastline to the east rises up to the spectacular towering cliffs of the Glamorgan Heritage Coast.

Southerndown

One of the few breaks in the 14-mile stretch of precipitous Heritage Coast cliffs occurs at Southerndown's Dunraven Bay - an attractive sandy beach which in 1993 won a Rural Beach Seaside Award from the Tidy Britain Group.

The sheltered beach offers safe bathing and good surfing, and has made Southerndown a popular little resort. There is also a Heritage Coast

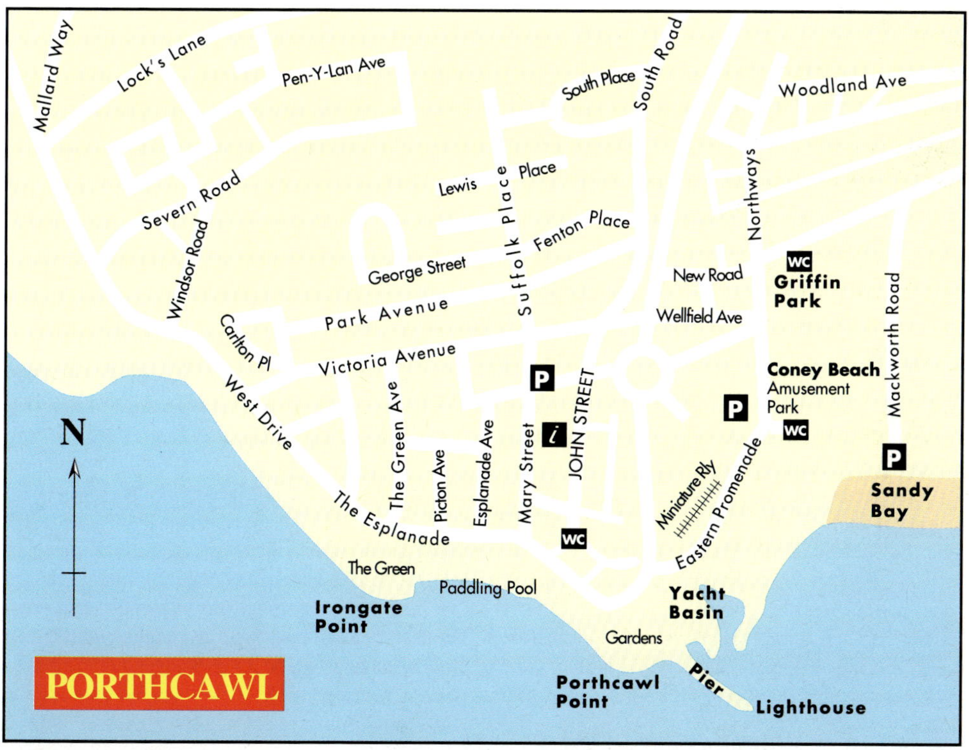

Porthcawl Funfair

Wales Tourist Board

Visitor Centre near the beach. From the centre you can explore Dunraven Park - 56 acres of sloping grasslands which were part of the estate of the now-demolished Dunraven Castle.

Bridgend

Medieval Bridgend is the largest town in Ogwr, 5 miles east of Porthcawl. Its position at the confluence of three rivers - the Llynfi, Ogmore and Garw - saw it grow as a market town and administrative centre for a wide area. It prospered further with the mining in the valleys to the north, and then survived the great decline in the coal industry. Today it is a thriving town with excellent shopping and leisure facilities.

The ancient fortress of Newcastle is at the centre of the old town, to the west of Bridgend, and the old bridge still spans the river.

Maesteg

The name Maesteg means Fair Meadow - a reflection of an attractive setting in the days before coal mining gripped the Llynfi Valley and Maesteg became another 19th century industrial town.

Situated near the head of the valley and surrounded by steep hills, Maesteg is renowned for its Friday open-air market. This is held next to the daily covered market in the shadow of the town hall, which with its clock tower is a very distinctive building. Another building of note is the restored blast furnace engine house which is home to Maesteg Sports Centre.

The road north out of the town climbs steeply before dropping down into the narrow Afan Valley, birthplace of Richard Burton. It is said that he made his acting debut on the stage of Maesteg Town Hall. It is also said that *Land of My Fathers*, later to become the Welsh national anthem, was first sung in public in Maesteg chapel.

Merthyr Mawr

This picturesque village is the perfect image of chocolate-box thatched cottages and rustic charm. In fact, it is an image of England rather than Wales. The village, with its church and green fields, is two miles south of Bridgend on the banks of the River Ogmore. It lies on the edge of the huge sand dune system of Merthyr Mawr Warren

- one of the biggest areas of dunes in Britain, and some of the highest in Europe. Iron Age and other important archaeological finds have been made here, and many are on display at the National Museum of Wales in Cardiff. A network of footpaths criss-crosses the dunes, which are an important wildlife habitat and a Site of Special Scientific Interest. Standing among the dunes are the sparse ruins of Candleston Castle.

Glamorgan Heritage Coast

Heritage Coast is a title given to the most beautiful, undeveloped stretches of coastline in England and Wales. But it is more than just a name: every section of Heritage Coast is protected because it is simply too precious to lose. Without this protection - and positive action to keep it unspoilt - the coastline would disappear mile by mile.

The Glamorgan Heritage Coast, one of seven in Wales, borders the Bristol Channel between Merthyr Mawr in the west and Aberthaw in the east. Within its 14-mile length it contains dramatic cliffs and unusual and surprisingly remote scenery.

Prevailing south-west winds are advancing the sand dunes of Merthyr Mawr, east of which rise the high yellow cliffs of banded limestone and shale. The cliffs, crumbling and highly unstable, run almost continuously along the entire Heritage Coast section, interrupted only occasionally by the shoreline, such as at Dunraven Bay.

The Heritage Coast Visitor Centre is located near the beach at Dunraven Bay, Southerndown, and further information is available there.

ATTRACTIONS & PLACES OF INTEREST

Bryngarw Country Park

Located just a few miles from the centre of Bridgend, secluded Bryngarw Country Park is a haven of natural beauty, wildlife and tranquility. This is the ideal place to get away from it all and enjoy the park's 113 acres of scenic contrasts - open meadows, thick woodland, immaculate gardens, ornamental lakelands and riverside walks. There are picnic areas, an adventure playground, a Visitor Centre, refreshments, exhibitions and special events, and the park's most

Dunraven Bay, South Heritage Coast

Wales Tourist Board

famous feature - the Japanese Garden. The park is open all through the year. For more information ring 0656 725155.

Candleston Castle

Candleston Castle was a 15th-century fortified manor house built on the edge of the Merthyr Mawr Warren. Very little of the house now remains.

Claypits Pottery

In addition to pottery, the Claypits workshop produces a range of gold and silver jewellery. Ring 0656 661733.

Coity Castle, Bridgend

An extensive ruin of an important medieval Norman stronghold, 2 miles north-east of Bridgend town centre. The castle dates from the 14th century.

Coney Beach Amusement Complex, Porthcawl

All the fun of the fair, with a big choice of great rides and amusements overlooking the beach. Ring 0656 713111.

Ewenny Pottery

The oldest working pottery in Wales, founded in 1610. Visit the workshops and showroom and see traditional skills at work in the creation of beautiful earthenware items. Ring 0656 653020.

Ewenny Priory

An unusual fortified 12th-century religious settlement, founded in 1141, which looks more like a castle than an abbey. It is considered to be one of the best examples of its kind in Britain.

Glamorgan Nature Centre

Located 2 miles south-west of Tondu, near Bridgend, the Nature Centre is the headquarters of Glamorgan Wildlife Trust and is rich in flora and fauna. While here you can become a member of the Trust and so make a contribution to important conservation work. Ring 0656 724100.

Grand Pavilion, Porthcawl

A popular seafront venue for summer shows and a wide variety of entertainment throughout the year. For information about the current programme ring 0656 716996.

Heritage Coast Centre, Southerndown

This visitor centre is situated near the beach and provides information about the 14-mile stretch of Glamorgan Heritage Coast, which begins at Newton, just east of Porthcawl. Ring 0656 880157.

Coity Castle

Wales Tourist Board

Kenfig Pool & Dunes National Nature Reserve

The sand dunes of the Kenfig Burrows and the reserve's 70-acre freshwater pool provide an important habitat for a variety of wildlife. More information about the reserve is available from the Visitor Centre, and there are also exhibitions and walks to enjoy. Ring 0656 743386.

Marlborough Military Models

The studios of the skilled craftspeople who create these finely-detailed model soldiers and figurines are open to the public. They are located at Pontycymer in the Garw Valley, east of Maesteg. Ring 0656 871774.

Ogmore Castle

Wales Tourist Board

Newcastle Castle, Bridgend

The remains of this Norman castle boast an exceptionally well-preserved south gateway, which is also notable for its richly-carved decoration. The castle stands on a hill overlooking the town and river.

Ogmore Castle

Ogmore Castle stands beside the River Ewenny and was a strategic Norman stronghold - part of a triangle of defences on the fertile Vale of Glamorgan. It was built to guard the ford, an important crossing point of the river, which is so shallow here that you can easily walk across on the stepping stones.

Porthcawl Museum

Located in John Street, this small museum has interesting displays of geological specimens, costumes and memorabilia of old Porthcawl. Ring 0656 712211.

Peter Wills Pottery & Gallery

Located at Newcastle Hill, Bridgend, along with the William Brown Studio. Ring 0656 662902.

The Welsh Porcelain Company, Maesteg

An interesting factory shop located on the Forge Estate. Ring 0656 734999.

William Brown Studio

A display of paintings and print-making at Newcastle Hill, Bridgend. Combine a trip here with a visit to the Peter Wills Pottery and Gallery. Ring 0656 650685.

SPORTS & ACTIVITIES

Ogwr provides an excellent choice of all-weather sports and leisure facilities.

Bridgend Recreation Centre

A multi-activity centre - the largest sports and leisure complex in South Wales. Its showpiece is the new leisure pool, featuring main and splash pools, a wave machine, waterslide, water cannon and toddlers' slide. Other major facilities include the 8-rink bowls hall (which converts to a roller skating rink during the summer), a large multi-purpose sports hall, gymnasium, squash courts, solarium, creche, and a choice of cafes and bars. There are also special attractions and soft play facilities for children, such as fun castles and a ball pool. For more information ring 0656 657491.

Garw Valley Centre, Pontycymer

A multi-purpose centre with a sports hall for badminton, volleyball, basketball, gymnastics and many other activities. The conditioning room has exercising and weight-training equipment, and other facilities include a sunbed and an area for keep fit. Ring 0656 870886.

Griffin Park Bowling Greens, Porthcawl

These immaculate greens regularly host top bowling competitions.

Llangeinor Swimming Pool

A first-class indoor pool, 25 metres long, ideal for serious swimmers. Ring 0656 870258.

Maesteg Golf Club

Ring 0656 732037.

Maesteg Sports Centre

An impressive centre which has a very novel reception area - a restored blast furnace engine house, dating from 1828, displaying many of its original features. The centre's facilities include a large sports hall, gymnasium, squash courts, fitness suite, snooker room and lounge bar. Ring 0656 737121.

Maesteg Swimming Pool

The facilities have been refurbished and upgraded and in addition to the main 25-metre pool and learner pool now include a sauna, steam rooms, sunbeds, whirlpool bath and rest area. Ring 0656 733073.

Mid Glamorgan Riding Club, nr Bridgend

Located at Heol-y-Cyw, the club offers you the opportunity to sample the delights of forest and mountain trekking through magnificent scenery. There is also an indoor school. Ring 0656 862959.

Ogwr Ridgeway Walk

A dramatic 13-mile countryside path across high ground, giving spectacular panoramic views - on a clear day as far as the hills of Somerset and Devon. For more information ring 0656 662141, extension 3806.

Ogmore Vale Swimming Pool

A popular 18-metre indoor pool. Ring 0656 840420.

Pencoed Swimming Pool

A 25-metre pool with a large spectator gallery, sunbeds and a sauna suite. Ring 0656 862360.

Pyle & District Leisure Centre

A social centre as well as a leisure centre, with multi-gym, keep fit classes, and floodlit outdoor 5-a-side pitch and tennis court. Ring 0656 743712.

Pyle and Kenfig Golf Club

Ring 0656 713093.

Pyle Swimming Pool

Here you will find a 25-metre pool, a steam room, sunbeds and a cafe. During school holidays there are fun sessions for children and courses in canoeing, snorkelling and water polo. Ring 0656 744019.

Royal Porthcawl Golf Club

Ring 0656 712251.

Southerndown Golf Club

Ring 0656 880326.

St. Mary's Hill Golf Club, Pencoed

Ring 0656 864720.

Ynysawdre Swimming Pool, Tondu

Keep fit classes, a creche, sauna suite, sunbeds and a multigym are all available here in addition to the 25-metre pool. Ring 0656 720806.

Brace Harvatt Associates

Exploring Further Afield

DINEFWR

The borough of Dinefwr (pronounced Din-ev-oor) was created as part of local government reorganisation in 1974. It is an area of 374 square miles, encompassing some of the most beautiful countryside in Wales, and it lies to the north of Swansea, touching the counties of Dyfed, West Glamorgan and Powys.

Dinefwr takes its name from the medieval castle sited on a rocky outcrop in the Vale of Towy, just a mile or so west of the market town of Llandeilo - the administrative centre of the borough, and once the county town of Carmarthenshire. There are two other towns in the borough - historic Llandovery and the more industrialised centre of Ammanford - and the majority of Dinefwr's 40,000 population live within these three towns.

Dinefwr has been described as the gateway to ancient Wales. It is a region of spectacular landscapes and Welsh culture, with a history so shrouded in the mists of time that it has become indistinguishable from folklore, myth and legend.

Dinefwr Castle was built in the 12th century. It was the stronghold of Rhys ap Gruffydd, who successfully resisted the English invaders until Edward I brought the struggle to a violent conclusion at the end of the 13th century. During the reign of Henry VIII, the descendants of Rhys moved out of Dinefwr Castle and into Newton House, a stately home nearby. Rebuilt in the 17th century, this is now owned by the National Trust and is being restored; part of the ground floor is already open to the public. The castle itself is owned by Dyfed Wildlife Trust and is being repaired by Cadw (Welsh Historic Monuments) to allow safe public access.

Mewslade Bay

John F Hendy

Dinefwr Castle is not the only magnificent medieval stronghold still surviving in the borough. One of the most dramatic is Carreg Cennen Castle, perched high on a rocky limestone crag 300 feet above the River Cennen. A few miles away is the hilltop ruin of Dryslwyn Castle, which stands within clear view of Paxton's Tower, a 19th-century folly. The town of Llandovery also has its castle ruin, overlooking the town's car park.

Visitors from Swansea need travel only 20 miles to reach the heart of Dinefwr. This is an area where you can find your own space: there are over 6 acres of countryside to every inhabitant - a fact readily apparent as you take in the sheer majesty of the scenery. The Cambrian Mountains rise to the north of the Vale of Tywi, while brooding to the south is the Black Mountain of the Brecon Beacons National Park. Birds of prey circle high above the landscape, among them the once-threatened red kite.

The Black Mountain, the Cambrians and the valleys of the Tywi and Cothi rivers are now the subject of signposted tours, designed to entice motorists off the beaten track. This is the way to discover the real Wales, taking you past such dramatic sights as the Llyn Brianne Reservoir - a man-made lake holding more than 13 billion gallons.

Helping to preserve the natural beauty of Dinefwr is a novel scheme called Tir Cymen (meaning Tidy Landscape). Under this scheme farmers receive a special payment to protect landscape, wildlife and archaeology, with extra incentive to preserve features such as ancient woodlands and field boundaries. Dinefwr is one of only three districts in Wales to be selected for the scheme.

Other great visitor attractions of Dinefwr are the Roman gold mines of Dolacouthi, near Pumpsaint, which are owned by the National Trust, and Gelli Aur Country Park, near Llandeilo, where you can enjoy a day exploring nature trails, a deer park and the famous arboretum.

Dinefwr is also noted for one other feature: its concentration of traditional Welsh craft workshops and studios. For example, in Llandeilo a co-operative known as Crafts Alive stocks hundreds of hand-made creations, both practical and decorative, and up river in Llandovery the former Meat Hall has been transformed into a new craft centre. In addition, the Trapp Arts & Crafts Centre has a shop and display area within its workshops. Many local artists and craftspeople also extend a warm welcome to visitors who wish to see them at work in their premises.

Further information about any of Dinefwr's many visitor attractions is available from the Borough Council's Tourism Office in Llandeilo. Ring 0558 822521, ext 268.

Canolfan Grefft Dinefwr

Y CREFFTAU GORAU DAN UN TO

Yng Nghanolfan Grefft Dinefwr, mae'r gorau o dan un to ... o gelficyn derw newydd sy'n dangos traddodiad canrifoedd, i lestri papier mache sy'n ysgafn, lliwgar a modern ... o nwyddau sy'n costio punt, i ddamau sy'n costio cannoedd.

Y bwriad yw rhoi profiad cyflawn o fyd crefft ... lle i daro i mewn iddo neu drculio awr neu ddwy. Does dim angen crywdro'r wlad i chwilio am gampweithiau ... arhoswch, a gweld y cyfan.

Y GEGIN ARDDOL
Ty bwyta sy'n cynnig bwyd iach ac awyrgylch braf. Mae'r fwydlen yn cynnig amrywiaeth o fwydydd lleol, gyda dewis llysieuol da. Llc am ginio hamddenol neu am gwpaned a chlonc.

**YR HEN FARCHNAD,
LLANYMDDYFRI,
DYFED SA20 0AA
FFON: 0550 21452
FFACS: 0550 21452**

Lle: Yng nghanol tre Llanymddyfri ar yr A40. Chwiliwch am gloc yfarchnad - mae'r Ganolfan yn union oddi tano!

Dinefwr Craft Centre

ALL THE BEST IN WELSH CRAFTS

Dinefwr Craft Centre is right at the heart of an old market town that is, itself, at the heart of South Wales - a meeting point for mountains and valleys and, now, for quality crafts.

A fully-rounded experience ... see craftspeople at work ... sample the area's best ... have a coffee or a meal in friendly, relaxed surroundings ... pop in or take your time.

THE KITCHEN GARDEN
Excellent, wholesome food in a pleasant atmosphere. We specialise in local foods with a wide choice of vegetarian dishes. For snacks or leisurely meals.

**THE OLD MARKET HALL,
LLANDOVERY,
DYFED SA20 0AA
TEL: 0550 21452
FAX: 0550 21452**

How to find us: At the centre of Llandovery on the A40. Look for the clock tower - we're directly underneath!

Dinefwr

John F Hendy

Llanddewi Church

PEMBROKESHIRE

Pembrokeshire is famous for many things. Its national park is the only coastal national park in Britain, drawing visitors from all over the world. Among its many attractions is the Castlemartin Peninsula, where erosion of the limestone cliffs has created a series of dramatic geological features such as sea caves, blowholes, arches and stacks. The Green Bridge of Wales, a natural arch, is a particularly well-known landmark of the peninsula.

The 186-mile Pembrokeshire Coast Path starts at Poppit Sands and runs right round to South Pembrokeshire in a virtually unbroken line, terminating at Amroth. On the way it skirts many fabulous beaches, including Whitesands, Broad Haven and Barafundle, and takes in the first-class resorts of Tenby and Saundersfoot.

North Pembrokeshire is the home of St David's, Britain's smallest city, and the wild and wonderful Preseli Hills. The offshore islands of Skomer, Skokholm, Ramsey and Grassholm provide sanctuary for colonies of gannets, puffins and the nocturnal Manx shearwaters. In the old county town of Haverfordwest, you can enjoy a bustling market and the attractive riverside shopping complex.

Dividing the north of the county from the south is the Haven Waterway, one of the world's finest natural deep-water harbours. It is well patronised by yachtsmen and watersport enthusiasts, who take full advantage of the facilities at Pembroke Dock and Lawrenny Quay and the marinas at Neyland and Milford Haven. From the upper reaches of the waterway - the Daugleddau estuary - stretch the Landsker Borderlands, one of the few inland areas within the national park and a rural retreat to delight all those who like to explore off the beaten track. At the heart of the Landsker Borderlands is Narberth, with its superb Landsker Visitor Centre.

In South Pembrokeshire, the magnificent medieval castles of Pembroke, Carew and Manorbier all have substantial ruins, Carew offering the added attraction of a Celtic cross and tidal mill. Pembroke Castle was the birthplace of Henry VII, and the historic town which grew up around it boasts an excellent new Visitor Centre. Nearby is Pembroke Dock, where you can catch the ferry to Rosslare in Ireland. Fishguard, in North Pembrokeshire, also operates a ferry service to Rosslare.

South Pembrokeshire's other big attractions include Caldey Island, just off Tenby, where Cistercian monks produce chocolate, perfume and yoghurt. And if you really want to have fun, don't miss a trip to Oakwood - Wales' biggest theme park.

CARMARTHENSHIRE

As well as marking the end of the Pembrokeshire Coast Path, Amroth sits on the border of Carmarthenshire. Carmarthen itself competes with Aberystwyth as the main shopping centre for West Wales. Its famous indoor and outdoor markets are alongside the shops of the old town and the shopping complex of the new, and many of the big-name stores are here. Yet Carmarthen, which among other things boasts a Roman amphitheatre, manages to retain its market-town charm and rural atmosphere - helped by the fact that Welsh is still widely spoken here.

Its county town aside, Carmarthenshire is best known today for the great Welsh poet Dylan Thomas. Born in Swansea, he lived the last years of his life at the Boat House in Laugharne, where his "water and tree room on the cliff" provided inspiration for much of his best work, including *Under Milk Wood.* The Boat House is now a fascinating Heritage Centre dedicated to Dylan's work. He died in New York in 1953, aged 39, and his grave in Laugharne's St Martin's churchyard is marked by a simple white cross, though there is also a plaque in his memory in Poets' Corner, Westminster Abbey.

Laugharne is a quaint medieval township, a status granted by royal charter in the 13th century, and still conducts its council business in accordance with ancient tradition. The castle, attractively set overlooking the Taf estuary, is currently being restored and was one of several in West Wales which captured Turner's imagination.

Close to Laugharne is Llanstephan Castle, an impressive ruin with superb views, and a little way along the coast is the popular resort of Pendine. The 7 miles of sands are famous in the annals of motor racing history. In the 1920's, Sir Malcolm Campbell set several world landspeed records here.

Just north of Carmarthen is the preserved Gwili Railway - unusual in Wales because its steam locomotives run on standard gauge track.

Carmarthenshire, which has many legends linking it with Merlin, the Arthurian wizard, is a beautiful county to explore by car, horseback or on foot. The valleys of the Teifi and Towy are very picturesque, and the Brechfa Forest is a favourite retreat for walkers.

Dinefwr, Pembrokeshire and Carmarthenshire are only three of the regions within easy distance of South Wales. Other areas to explore include Brecon Beacons and the Irfon Valley, Ceredigion, Rhymney Valley, the valleys of the Rhondda, and the Vale of Glamorgan. Each is different, and each has enough character and attractions to satisfy even the most curious visitor.

Cenarth

The National Trust

The National Trust has a very strong presence in South Wales, owning and managing over 50,000 acres of countryside and 82 miles of coastline. This includes ten per cent of the total area of the Gower Peninsula, and more than two thirds of its coastline.

In addition, the Trust has a number of visitor attractions located across the region, several of which have already been described in preceding pages - namely Aberdulais Falls and Henryhd Falls in the Vale of Neath, and Rhossili and Pennard Cliffs on Gower.

The following is a guide to other important National Trust sites in South and West Wales.

DINEFWR PARK

At the heart of Welsh history for a thousand years, the park took shape as we see it today in the years after 1775, when the medieval castle, house, gardens, woods and deer park were integrated into one vast and beautiful landscape. Footpaths through the estate lead to Dinefwr Castle, Llandyfeisant Church (owned by the Dyfed Wildlife Trust) and outstanding views of the Towy Valley. There is also an exhibition and video on the ground floor of Newton House, which is currently undergoing major repair work.

DOLAUCOTHI ROMAN GOLD MINES, DINEFWR

One of only three gold mines in the entire Roman empire, the 2000-year-old Dolaucothi mine is today owned by the National Trust. It is set in wooded hills overlooking the beautiful Cothi Valley, near Pumpsaint on the A482, midway between Lampeter and Llanwrda. You can enjoy a guided tour of the underground workings and walk along the Miners' Way. There is also an information centre and a National Trust shop.

The mines, first exploited by the Romans 2000 years ago, have a fascinating history. The Miners' Way walk gives superb views across the estate, and you can don a miner's helmet lamp for a guided tour of the underground workings and experience what life must have been like for the miners during the 1930's.

MWNT, CEREDIGION

Beautiful, unspoilt and isolated, yet easily accessible, Mwnt is in the care of the National Trust and is a sheer delight for anyone looking for an alternative to the more populated resorts of Cardigan Bay. Mwnt's wonderful charm is that it offers three attractions in one very small area. There is a fine sheltered beach lying below the cliffs; a 250 ft hill which gives magnificent coastal views, and from which the place takes its name (Mwnt in Welsh is Traeth y Munt - the Beach of the Mound); and the tiny medieval Church of the Holy Cross, which dates from around 1400 and occupies an earlier Celtic site.

So on reaching Mwnt you have the choice of going up the steep path to the top of the mount, where the panoramic views are worth the effort, or down the zigzagging steps to the beach. These steps take you past an old limekiln - a reminder of the days when limestone was landed here and manhandled up the slope to avoid the extortionate tolls imposed on the turnpike roads.

The superb beach is a small sandy cove which faces west and is protected from winds by the headland. So it is a natural sun trap and idyllic in summer. Less appealing, though, is the idea that in 1155 a battle was fought here between the Welsh and the Flemings. The home forces successfully repelled the invaders - a victory which, until the turn of the 19th century, was celebrated with an annual mock battle held on the first Sunday in January, known as Sul Coch (Bloody Sunday).

The isolated position of the whitewashed medieval Holy Cross Church (Eglwys y Graig) means that it was obscured from the view of passing seaborne raiders, for whom churches and their treasures were rich targets. It is probable that pilgrims landed at Mwnt in the sixth and seventh centuries on their way to Bardsey Island, the traditional burial ground of the Celtic saints.

PENBRYN, CEREDIGION

Lying below the wooded cliffs that extend between Llangrannog and Tresaith is the long,

golden beach of Penbryn. Penbryn itself nestles half a mile inland, in the picturesque valley of the little River Hoffnant. The area is very attractive for its cliff walks and beaches, and in summer boasts a great variety of butterflies, such as meadow brown, common skipper, peacock, common blue, tortoise-shell and others. The mysterious hillside church of St. Michael's is thought to be one of the oldest in Wales. Among its many curious features are a weeping chancel, a leper squint and a sacramental cup dated 1574. Legend has it that the walls of the graveyard are circular so that there are no corners for the Devil to hide in, and it is also said that when an attempt was made to rebuild the church on another site, the stones were miraculously returned to this ancient site overnight. Such stories support the idea that the area has been occupied for many centuries. Iron Age and Romano-British remains have been uncovered, and on the cliff top between Penbryn and Tresaith is the remnant of a hillfort. There is also an inscribed standing stone at Dyffryn Bern, a short distance inland, under which was found a gold coin dating from the first century AD and a burial urn. Weapons and bones have also been discovered close by.

Other National Trust attractions are to be found in Pembrokeshire (Colby Woodland Garden, the Stackpole Estate, the Tudor Merchant's House Tenby, the Marloes Peninsula and St. David's Peninsula); Monmouth (The Kymin); and 10,000 acres of the Brecon Beacons.

NATIONAL TRUST MEMBERSHIP

As a registered charity, the National Trust receives no government funding and relies almost entirely on voluntary contributions. If you would like to help safeguard our beautiful countryside and historic buildings of national importance - for our own enjoyment now and the benefit of future generations - please support us by becoming a member of the National Trust today. You can join at any of the properties mentioned above, or by contacting the Public Affairs Department, The National Trust, The King's Head, Llandeilo, Dyfed SA19 6BB. Tel: 0558 822800.

Accommodation & Eating Out

LLANELLI

LLWYNIFAN FARM, Llangennech, Llanelli. 1 mile junction 48 M4. Central for touring for visiting any part of South Wales. Caravan club members only, and bookings only. **Tel: (0554) 820420**

SWANSEA & THE MUMBLES

ACORNS HOUSE, Gower Road, Sketty, Swansea. Situated on the gateway to Gower. Bedrooms well appointed, some en suite. Decorated to a high standard. Colour TV. Licensed. Parking. **Tel: (0792) 201345**

BELMONT GUEST HOUSE, 2 Mirador Crescent, Uplands, Swansea. B&B, TV, tea/coffee, car park. **Tel: (0792)466812**

DEVON VIEW HOTEL, 396 Oystermouth Road. Seafront family run hotel offering homely atmosphere and good food. Satellite colour TV and video, tea/coffee facilities in all rooms. Free parking. **Tel: (0792) 462008**

HOME FROM HOME, 2a Queen's Road, Mumbles. We have a wide range of houses, flats, cottages and chalets to let for self-catering holidays throughout the year. Short breaks available in Spring & Autumn. Please phone for a colour brochure. **Tel: (0792) 360624**

JEZREEL GUEST HOUSE, 168 Bishopston Road. Gower Coast small guest house B&B, easy reach of beaches and countryside. Hot and cold in rooms and tea making facilities. Large parking area on drive. Lounge with TV and separate dining room. WTBH **Tel: 0792 232744**

RIVERSIDE CARAVAN PARK, Morriston. Flat level riverside setting, superb modern facilities 90% electrical hook-up. Indoor heated swimming pool, licensed club, games rooms, childrens play area. Ideal location for all West Wales attractions, Swansea, Mumbles & Gower, Vale of Neath. Situated 200 yards from Junc 45 of M4. Graded Park 4444 **Tel: (0792) 775587**

SWANSEA BEACH HOTEL, 390 Oystermouth Road. Seafront, lounge, central heating, hot and cold, colour TV all rooms and satellite link, bed and breakfast, snacks and evening meals available on request. **Tel: (0792) 655105**

THE COAST HOUSE, 708 Mumbles Road, Mumbles. On the seafront, overlooking the magnificent views of Swansea Bay, the Coast House has several en suite bedrooms. All bedrooms have sea-views, TV and tea making facilities. Family run. Bed and Breakfast only. **Tel: (0792) 368702**

TY REBECCA, Cwmcile Farm, Salem, Morriston. Ty Rebecca is 300 years old. The original farmhouse on a dairy and sheep farm extensively renovated. During the Rebecca riots in 1843 Captain John Napier, Chief Constable of Glamorgan was assaulted at Ty Rebecca by the Morgan Family. G.C.H. colour TV in lounge, 1D, 1TW, 1S all with H.C. **Tel: (0792) 845141**

WINDSOR LODGE HOTEL, 15 Mount Pleasant, Swansea. Windsor Lodge is a grade II listed Georgian building near the City Centre. The 18 rooms are en suite and newly refurbished. We are one of the AA's top 20 one star hotels in the U.K. **Tel: 0792 648996**

THE GOWER PENINSULA

CULVERHOUSE HOTEL & RESTAURANT, Port Eynon, Gower. Peacefully situated with superb coast and countryside. Quality service and fabulous food in our licensed restaurant and tea-rooms. Most rooms en suite with seaview. Pets welcome. **Tel: (0792) 390755**

GOWER HOLIDAY VILLAGE, Scurlage. Holiday bungalows ideally located for enjoying the scenic beauty of the Gower. Heated indoor swimming pool, jacuzzi, sauna, solarium, games room, putting green, playground, launderette, shops, hairdressers. Day visitors welcome. **Tel: (0792) 390431**

HEATHERLANDS, 1 Hael Lane, Southgate, Gower. B&B, cliffs, beaches walking distance. 3 bedrooms H + C, tea making facilities, shower room 1 en suite, TV, lounge and parking. **Tel: (0792) 233256**

NICHOLASTON HOUSE HOTEL, Nicholaston, Gower. Country house hotel set in it's own beautiful grounds. All 13 rooms en suite, colour TV, tea/coffee facilities. A la carte restaurant, weddings/parties, up to 120 catered for. Full size snooker table. Residents lounge. **Tel: (0792) 371317**

PARC LE BREOS HOUSE, Parkmill, Gower. Secluded 19thC farmhouse, B&B, evening meal optional, mostly en suite bedrooms, TV, lounge, games room. Homegrown food, warm welcome, safe lawn play area; ideal touring, footpath to Three Cliffs Bay/Cefn Bryn, Pony trekking/paddock rides available. **Tel: (0792) 371636**

PITTON CROSS CARAVAN AND CAMPING PARK, Rhossili, Gower. Spectacular views to Lundy Island, Brecon Beacons. Flat site, good access, near to beaches, foot paths. **Open April - October. Tel: 0792 390593**

SUMMERCLIFFE CHALET PARK, Gower. Self catering chalets in quiet select park. Fully equipped sleeping 2 - 6, 300 yds from Caswell Bay's beautiful beach. **Tel: 0792 758091**

THE MEADOWS, Llanmadoc, Gower. Beautiful self-contained apartment sleeps four + cot. Wing of magnificent bungalow in large grounds with panoramic coastal views. WTB highest grading for quality. Central heating, bed linen, colour TV, freezer, washer/dryer, microwave. **Tel: (0792) 386346**

WESTERNSIDE FARM BUNGALOWS, Horton, Gower. Two bedroom, centrally heated, sleep 4. Set on quiet park overlooking Port Eynon Bay. Perfect base for exploring Gower. WTB 4 Dragons. **For full details Tel: (0792) 371301**

WOODSIDE GUEST HOUSE, Oxwich, Gower, Swansea SA3 1LS. Our 200 year old converted cottage offers en suite accommodation and Welsh cuisine served in our beamed dining room and bar with inglenook fireplace. WTB 2 Crowns commended. Les Routier recommended. **Diane and David Workman Tel: (0792) 390791**

PORT TALBOT

TY'N-Y-CAEAU, Margam Village, Port Talbot. B&B + self catering, bath or shower en suite, WTB 2 crowns commended, colour TV and tea making facilities, original 17th Cent Vicarage near Jct 38 M4, Margam Park and Abbey. **Tel: (0639) 883897**

EXPLORING FURTHER AFIELD

THE PLOUGH INN at RHOSMAEN, Llandeilo, Dyfed SA19 6NP. Restaurant & bar meals, afternoon teas. En suite accommodation. 4 Crowns, highly commended. Conference facilities. Gym & sauna. **Tel: 0558 823431**

GALLERY

ATTIC GALLERY, 61 Wind Street, Swansea. Wales longest established privately run gallery. There is a changing display of new paintings, original prints and sculpture by leading artists. Regular programme of exhibitions. **Open: Mon - Fri 10 - 5, Sat 10 - 4. Tel: (0792) 653387**

Index

Page numbers in **bold** refer to illustrations.

A
Aberavon 70
Aberdulais Falls **49**, 54, 59-61
Afan Argoed **72**
Afan Argoed Country Park 73
Afan Lido 71
Afan Lido Concert Hall 75
Afan Lido Leisure Complex 75
Afan Valley 72
Attic Gallery 33
B
Baglan 67
Beaches
- Aberavon 10
- Bluepool Bay 10
- Bracelet Bay 6
- Brandy Cove 7
- Broughton Bay 10
- Caswell Bay 6, **11**
- Cefn Sidan Sands 5, **18**
- Crawley 9
- Fall Bay 9
- Horton 9
- Langland Bay 6
- Limeslade Bay 6
- Llanelli 5
- Llanginnith 10
- Margam 10
- Merthyr Mawr 10, 80
- Mewslade Bay 9, **85**
- Mumbles 6, **47**
- Ogmore-By-Sea 11, 79
- Oxwich Bay **5**, 9
- Pebbles Bay 7
- Pembrey 5
- Penmaen 7
- Port Eynon 9. 45, **44**
- Pwll-du Bay 7
- Rest Bay 10, **78**
- Rhossili 9, 41
- Rotherslade Bay 6
- Sandy Bay 10
- Southerndown 11, 79
- Trecco Bay 10
- Tor Bay 7
- Three Cliffs Bay **8**, 9, **9**
- Whiteford 10

Bishops' Wood Countryside Centre 48
Blaengwynfi **70**
Brangwyn Hall 31, 32
Bridgend 80
Bryngarw Country Park 81
Bryn Mill Park 33
Burry Port 17
C
Carmarthenshire 90
Castles
- Candleton 82
- Coity 82, **82**
- Kidwelly 13, 20
- Margam 69, **69,** 73
- Newcastle 83
- Ogmore 83, **83**
- Oystermouth 27, 33
- Pennard **46**
- Weobley 47

Cefn Bryn 38
Claypits Pottery 82
Clyne Farm Activity Centre 33
Clyne Gardens 33
Clyne Valley Country Park 33
Coal & Steam Centre **63**
Coney Beach Amusement Complex 82
Craft Workshop & Pottery (The 32)
Craig Gwladus Country Park **53**, 63
Crymlyn Bog National Nature Reserve 33
Cwmafan 69
Cwmdonkin Park 33
D
Dai the Dragon's Adventure World 17
Dan-Yr-Ogof Show Caves 64, **65**
Dinefwr 85-87, **88**
Dinefwr Park 91
Dolaucothi Roman Gold Mines 91
Dunraven Bay 79, **81**
E
Eaglebush Valley 63
Ewenny Pottery 82
Ewenny Priory 82
F
Furnace Pond 16
Furnace (The) 16
G
Glamorgan Heritage Coast 81
Glamorgan Heritage Coast Visitor Centre 82
Glamorgan Nature Centre 82
Glyn Vivian Art Gallery 31
Gnoll Country Park 54, 63
Golf
- Ashburnham 22
- Earlswood 64

Glyn Clydach House Hotel 64
Glynneath 64
Gnoll Park 64
Maesteg 75
Neath 64
Pembrey 22
Pontnewydd 21
Pyle & Kenfig 75
Royal Porthcawl 75
St Mary's Hill, Pencoed 84
Southerndown 84
Swansea Bay 64, 75
Tycroes 22
Grand Pavilion, Porthcawl 82
Grand Theatre, Swansea 25, 31
Gunsmoke Cowboy Town 59
H
Hwyrnos 32
K
Kenfig Pool and Dunes National Nature Reserve 82
Kidwelly 20
L
Llanddewi Church **89**
Llanelli Entertainment Centre 17
Llanelli Leisure Centre 14, 20
Llanelli Market 17
Llanrhidian **41**
Loughor Estuary **4**
Lovespoon Gallery (The) 33
M
Maesteg 80
Margam 67
Margam Country Park 73, **74**
Marlborough Military Models 83
Melincourt Falls 54, 59
Merthyr Mawr 80
Museums
Cefn Coed Colliery Museum 59
Maritime & Industrial Musem 31
Neath Borough Museum 63
Porthcawl Museum 83
Swansea Museum 31
Welsh Miner's Museum 73
Mwnt 91
N
National Eisteddfod 54-57
National Trust Visitor Centre, Rhossili 48
Neath Abbey 62, **62**
Neath Canal, Resolven 61
P
Pant-y-Sais Fen 64
Parc Howard **13**, 16
Pembrey Country Park 18
Pembrokeshire 89
Penbryn 91-92
Penclacwydd Wildfowl & Wetlands Centre 15
Penscynor Wildlife Park 57-59
People's Park 16
Plantasia 27, 31
Pontneddfechan 62
Pontrhydyfen Viaduct **68**, 73
Port-Eynon 9, **44,** 45
Port-Eynon Church **45**
Princess Royal Theatre 75
R
Rest Bay **78**
S
St Catherine's Church, Baglan 74
Sandy Water Park 16
Singleton Park **26**, 33
Small World Pony Centre 47
Stradey Park 14
Swansea Arts Workshop & Gallery 32
Swansea Bike Path 36
Swansea Laser Quest 33
Swansea Leisure Centre 34
Swansea Marina **23**, 25, **25**
Swansea Maritime Quarter 23, 31
Swansea Market 25, 31, **32**
Swansea Tourist Information Centre 30, 96
Swimming Pools
Afan Lido* 75
Bridgend Recreation Centre 83
Glynneath 65
Llanelli Leisure Centre 22
Llangatwg School 65
Llangeinor 83
Maesteg 84
Neath Leisure Centre 65
Ogmore Vale 84
Pencoed 84
Pyle 84
Swansea Leisure Centre 34
Ynysawdre, Tondu 84
Swiss Valley 16
T
Taibach 67
Taliesin Arts Centre 32
Three Cliffs Bay **8**
Tollgate Park 74
Tonna **52**
W
Welsh Miners Museum 73
Welsh Motorsports Centre 18
Worms Head **39**
Y
Y Felin Ddwr Mill & Craft Centre 48
Ystradfellte Falls **51**, 54

TOURIST INFORMATION CENTRES

Tourism Office
Llanelli Borough Council
Ty Elwyn, Llanelli SA15 3AP
Tel: 0554 742178

Tourist Information Centre
The Public Library, Vaughan Street
Llanelli SA15 3AS
Tel: 0554 772020

Tourist Information Centre
Pont Abraham, Junction 49 (M4)
Tel: 0792 883838

Tourist Information Centre
Singleton Street
Swansea SA1 3QG (city centre)
Tel: 0792 468321

Tourist Information Centre
Mumbles (Swansea Bus Station)
Tel: 0792 361302

Tourist Information Centre
Neath Borough Council
Civic Centre, Neath SA11 3QZ
Tel: 0639 641121 ext 277

Tourist Information Centre
Pontneddfechan, Vale of Neath
Tel: 0639 721795

Tourist Information Centre
Aberdulais, Neath
Tel: 0639 633531

Tourist Information Centre
Bagle Brook, Baglan, Port Talbot
Tel: 0639 823049

Porthcawl Tourist Information Centre
Department SB92
The Old Police Station, John Street
Porthcawl CF36 3DT
Tel: 0656 786639/782211

ACKNOWLEDGEMENTS

Many people have helped in the production of this guide. In particular I would like to thank Miles Cowsill, Linda Cowsill and Pat Somner of Lily Publications; Brace Harvatt Associates; Ian Smith of Bezier Design; Marilyn Gardner of Waterfront Graphics; John Hendy; Harcourt Litho; the Wales Tourist Board; Tonia Kemp and Swansea City Council; Ioan Evans and the staff of Llanelli Borough Council's Tourism Department; Clare Kendrick of Llanelli Leisure Centre; Steve Jones and the Borough of Port Talbot; Eleri Twynog Davies, Marketing Officer of the National Eisteddfod; John Churchill of the River Tawe Barrage project, Swansea; Neath Borough Council; Ogwr Borough Council; Dinefwr Borough Council; the National Trust; the staff of all the Tourist Information Centres listed in the guide; the British Tourist Authority; the Countryside Council for Wales; the Countryside Commission; the Tidy Britain Group; Gloria Hunniford; and - last but not least - to all the advertisers for their generous support.

PUBLISHERS

Lily Publications, 12 Millfields Close, Pentlepoir, Kilgetty, Pembrokeshire, Wales. SA68 0SA. Tel: (0834) 811895 Fax: (0834) 814484

PHOTOGRAPHY

All pictures unless credited are the work of Miles Cowsill, Lily Publications.